Marketing in a Web 2.0 World

Using Social Media, Webinars, ~~Blogs~~ ~~and~~ More
to Boost Your Sm~~all~~ ~~Business~~ ~~on a Budget~~

chptr 1+2
" 3+4
5+6
7

By Peter VanRysdam,
CMO of 352 Media Group

Foreword By Brian Goldfarb,
Director, Developer Platform Marketing
for Microsoft Corporation

MARKETING IN A WEB 2.0 WORLD — USING SOCIAL MEDIA, WEBINARS, BLOGS, AND MORE TO BOOST YOUR SMALL BUSINESS ON A BUDGET

Library of Congress Cataloging-in-Publication Data

VanRysdam, Peter, 1978-
  Marketing in a Web 2.0 world : using social media, webinars, blogs, and more to boost your small business on a budget / by Peter VanRysdam.
     p. cm.
  Includes bibliographical references and index.
  ISBN-13: 978-1-60138-317-4 (alk. paper)
  ISBN-10: 1-60138-317-7 (alk. paper)
  1. Internet marketing. 2. Communication in marketing. 3. Social media--Marketing. 4. Web 2.0. I. Title.
  HF5415.1265.V356 2010
  658.8'72--dc22
                                                2010014280

Printed in the United States

PROJECT MANAGER: Erin Everhart • eeverhart@352media.com
PEER REVIEWER: Marilee Griffin • mgriffin@atlantic-pub.com
ASSISTANT EDITOR: Shannon McCarthy • smccarthy@atlantic-pub.com
INTERIOR; PRE PRESS & PRODUCTION DESIGN: Samantha Martin • smartin@atlantic-pub.com
FRONT COVER DESIGN: Meg Buchner • meg@megbuchner.com
BACK COVER DESIGN: Jackie Miller • millerjackiej@gmail.com

Printed on Recycled Paper

We recently lost our beloved pet "Bear," who was not only our best and dearest friend but also the "Vice President of Sunshine" here at Atlantic Publishing. He did not receive a salary but worked tirelessly 24 hours a day to please his parents. Bear was a rescue dog that turned around and showered myself, my wife, Sherri, his grandparents Jean, Bob, and Nancy, and every person and animal he met (maybe not rabbits) with friendship and love. He made a lot of people smile every day.

We wanted you to know that a portion of the profits of this book will be donated to The Humane Society of the United States. *–Douglas & Sherri Brown*

The human-animal bond is as old as human history. We cherish our animal companions for their unconditional affection and acceptance. We feel a thrill when we glimpse wild creatures in their natural habitat or in our own backyard.

Unfortunately, the human-animal bond has at times been weakened. Humans have exploited some animal species to the point of extinction.

The Humane Society of the United States makes a difference in the lives of animals here at home and worldwide. The HSUS is dedicated to creating a world where our relationship with animals is guided by compassion. We seek a truly humane society in which animals are respected for their intrinsic value, and where the human-animal bond is strong.

Want to help animals? We have plenty of suggestions. Adopt a pet from a local shelter, join The Humane Society and be a part of our work to help companion animals and wildlife. You will be funding our educational, legislative, investigative and outreach projects in the U.S. and across the globe.

Or perhaps you'd like to make a memorial donation in honor of a pet, friend or relative? You can through our Kindred Spirits program. And if you'd like to contribute in a more structured way, our Planned Giving Office has suggestions about estate planning, annuities, and even gifts of stock that avoid capital gains taxes.

Maybe you have land that you would like to preserve as a lasting habitat for wildlife. Our Wildlife Land Trust can help you. Perhaps the land you want to share is a backyard—that's enough. Our Urban Wildlife Sanctuary Program will show you how to create a habitat for your wild neighbors.

So you see, it's easy to help animals. And The HSUS is here to help.

THE HUMANE SOCIETY
OF THE UNITED STATES.

2100 L Street NW • Washington, DC 20037 • 202-452-1100
www.hsus.org

ACKNOWLEDGEMENTS

Thank you to the staff at Atlantic Publishing Group, especially my editor, Erin Everhart, for all of her hard work and long hours making this book a reality. Thank you to Samantha Martin, Holly Gibbs, Meg Buchner, and Michelle Brownstein for their graphic design and layout help, which turned my words into a piece of art. Thank you to all of the contributors who shared their stories of success, as well as lessons learned; their input helped make the case studies valuable learning resources for small business owners. And finally, thank you to all of my coworkers at 352 Media Group for their feedback along the way.

WEB 2.0 WORLD

DEDICATION

To my Dad, for teaching me everything I know about business.

To my Mom, who taught me honesty and ethics.

To Megan and Abby, for their support during my long nights and weekends writing.

To Geoff, for giving me a shot.

Thanks.

TABLE OF CONTENTS

WEB 2.0 WORLD

Chapter 3: Making Your Website Truly Interactive   61

Chapter 4: Getting Search Engines to Notice Your Site   83

Chapter 5: The Benefits of a Business Blog   113

Chapter 6: Stop Talking, Start Listening — Social Networks as Focus Groups   135

Chapter 7: Joining — Not Controlling — The Conversation 165

Chapter 8: Building Your Network 189

Chapter 9: Establish Yourself as an Expert Online   223

Chapter 10: PR 2.0: Moving Past the Press Release   237

FOREWORD

"If u cant get ur msg across in 140 letters or less, then I probably don't care what you say. I wish this #foreword was that short #fb"

As we move into a world of community, grass-roots, socially integrated marketing that is powered by the Internet, marketers must begin to internalize the challenging concepts of less is more — concise is powerful. I am a marketer. Since 2003, I have marketed to developers and designers, the very people who not only embody Web 2.0, but those who helped create it. These customers tend to be on the bleeding edge of new-age marketing. Reaching them requires playing by new rules, and even though I work for a giant software company, these "new rules" dictate that I operate just like the stories you will read within the pages of *Marketing in a Web 2.0 World — Using Social Media, Webinars, Blogs, and More to Boost Your Small Business on a Budget.*

In my business, people say "marketing" is taboo. You will hear things like, "You don't 'market' to a developer or designer. Marketing is blasphemy." The truth, however, is that you do "market" to developers, just not in traditional ways. What is exciting for me is that the methods I have employed for years are now becoming the new staple for marketing to the broader set of customers; these are the exact techniques that you will learn about in this book.

Over the last seven years, I have seen massive changes in the way savvy marketers use technology. Each new advancement in technology that eventually goes mainstream leads to a subsequent change in consumer behavior that opens the doors to a variety of new ways to interact with and reach customers. These advancements impact my market first, and we have been forced to react sooner. First, it was through the need of a rich, interactive web presence. We had to build Web properties that had the right pre-sales information, and ones that acted as a hub for learning and social engagement. This meant we had to have fresh content that helped our customers be successful and engage them through blogs and forums. We built an online world where our customers could interact with each other, answer questions, receive recognition, and simultaneously deliver the marketing messages and brand power we were seeking. The ecosystem of customers became the channel for delivering our story, a channel that was more credible than any internal voice could ever be.

Second, we had to get smart about search. We saw that the majority of our customers found the location of their information from search engines. That meant focusing tons of energy on search engine optimization, friendly URLs, link ranking, keyword content, and usability. As marketers, we focused our energy on making sure that when someone asked Google a question, our website was the answer. And that the answer was usable, attractive, and easy to navigate for a large community.

Third, we had to go social. The "social graph," the complex set of connections (followers, friends, fans, etc.) that one has online, has massive potential for reach. A link that gets posted to Twitter that gets retweeted 100 times could hit 25,000 to 100,000 potential customers in seconds. You have to integrate the social concepts directly into your Web properties and marketing. Connect traditional marketing to digital and scale your message through the graph.

The beauty of a Web community, being smart about search, and going social is that this is cheap to do with the right dedication and a few tips and tricks. *Marketing in a Web 2.0 World* has everything you need to know to help propel your business (and your marketing prowess) into the Web 2.0 era and turn what may feel like toys for geeks and kids into real business results.

Brian Goldfarb (@bgoldy)
Director, Developer Marketing
Microsoft Corporation

Brian Goldfarb is the Director of Product Management for Developer Platforms at Microsoft. Goldfarb and his team are focused on product planning, business strategy, and global marketing for the platforms that developers and designers use for building the next generation of applications for Windows, the Web, and devices including Silverlight, .NET, IIS, and more. The platforms team also manages vertical efforts in the media, advertising, and enterprise space as it relates to our UX technologies like Silverlight and WPF. Goldfarb graduated with degrees in computer science and economics from Duke University.

INTRODUCTION

The Game has not Changed, Just the Venue

"If anything is certain, it is that change is certain. The world we are planning for today will not exist in this form tomorrow."

- Philip Crosby, author of *Quality is Free*

I do not know what a slide rule does. My father would tell me about using his as a kid every time he helped me with my math homework, but I grew up in an age where the slide rule was taught in history class, not math. In fact, we were not only allowed but actually encouraged to use calculators during exams by the time I reached high school — which might explain why math has never been my forte.

Marketing has undergone a similar transition during the first decade of the 21st century, thanks to technology advancements. Billboards have been replaced by websites, direct mail by online newsletters, and focus groups by social networking. All of the former tools still exist, but do not have quite the same impact as they once did. But they do have one thing the latter mediums do not: high costs. The cost of a billboard rental on the interstate for just one month is roughly that of creating a basic website. Printing a catalog once can cost ten times that of a good e-mailing service, and that is not even considering postage. Social networks give you unfiltered access to the opinions of millions of consumers in a matter of seconds — something a focus group could never hope to accomplish. Relationship marketing has evolved.

Advancements within the marketing community have resulted in two main benefits: unprecedented access to customers (as well as prospects) and dramatically lower costs to reach those audiences. Reaching a business-to-consumer (B2C) demographic during the second half of the 20th century meant producing high-dollar television and radio commercials and paying even higher amounts for the air time to run them. Despite the big budgets marketers shelled out, it was virtually impossible to reach a targeted demographic. Other options like print advertising and direct mail carried similar limitations and costs.

Business-to-business (B2B) marketers faced similar challenges, often focusing on trade publications and expensive expos and trade shows. The result was a clear advantage for large businesses that had the buying power to fund their growth. Without taking considerable risks with their marketing budgets or getting very lucky with their public relations efforts, small businesses had little opportunity to reach customers outside their local marketing. Budget marketing meant staying local or running the smallest national advertisement available. During that era, the large companies held all the chips.

The emergence of the Internet as a marketing tool has triggered a power shift from the company to the consumer. Social networks give customers a voice they never had until today. Through Web 2.0 technologies — a term that emerged in the early 2000s to describe interactive elements like forums, blogs, and user-generated content — an unsatisfied customer today has access to the tools to tell his or her story and actually impact a company's bottom line. Now, small businesses have a medium that allows them to easily reach customers on a national or even global scale. And getting that message out to millions of buyers — something that might have cost a small business's entire annual marketing budget — can in many cases only cost their staff's time and energy.

It is no surprise small businesses stand to benefit the most from the low-cost marketing options available through Web 2.0. Reach and cost, the two biggest roadblocks facing small companies, have all but eroded, leveling the playing field with larger competitors. The most important shift, though, is not from large to small businesses but instead from businesses to the consumers. Tools like Facebook and Twitter allow customers to share with each other their experiences, both positive and negative, with companies and products in real time. This has put the customer in control to a level that was unthinkable in the heyday of direct marketing in the late 1900s. Smaller, more adaptable, companies stand to benefit the most from this paradigm shift.

One frustration I have always experienced in reading business books is the focus on large businesses in case studies and examples. While it is often easier to quantify the results of a major enterprise's marketing endeavors, there are rarely actionable takeaways for the small business marketer working within a budget. Anyone can have success given the right tools, most notably a large marketing team and budget, but that rarely describes the readers' situation. That is why this book will focus on what the most important opportunity Web 2.0 has provided: It is the ability to make a big splash with little or no out-of-pocket expense. This book will not only introduce you to the tools available through Web 2.0, but will focus on those that give you the most impact for the smallest cost. In addition, the case studies presented will consist of other small organizations with success stories that can be put in to use in your business right away.

As the Chief Marketing Officer of 352 Media Group, not only have I been involved with marketing my Web development business, but I also know the difficulties of working with a limited budget. As one of the founders of 352 Media Group, I helped us grow from a three-person business selling

$49 websites to a 50-person company with clients ranging from Microsoft and American Express to the frame shop down the street. As a privately held company with no outside investment, we have done it all with a keen eye on the bottom line. The reason we survived the dot-com bust at the end of the 1990s is while other start-ups were putting up plasma screens in their in-office fitness centers, we were analyzing every decision ad nauseam because it was our money on the line. As a result, no campaign proceeded without us knowing it would bring a return. Sure, we took risks, but only when we had no other options.

While we are bigger today, we still have the same approach when it comes to marketing. I do not know why anyone would consider spending his or her entire year's budget on one television ad or a full-page spread in a national newspaper. Instead, Web 2.0 lets us reach the same people for far less money and in some cases none at all. (It does not hurt that I have 30 or so Web designers and programmers down the hall who can bring my ideas to life, but while it is better than hiring outside help, using those resources still costs the company money.) My experience has forced me to try virtually every tool available to marketers in the Web 2.0 era, good, bad, or indifferent. I have had some great successes as a result along with my share of flops, but most important is what I learned along the way. Now I hope that information can help you as you grow your business.

It is truly an exciting time to be in marketing in a small business. We have witnessed the transition from the slide rule to the calculator, the postcard to the e-mail newsletter, and even the billboard to the website. Now it is time to take the next step by implementing these new tools in our own businesses. The fact that you are reading this book is evidence you are ready to move past the "tried and true" promotional strategies and embrace budget marketing, version 2.0.

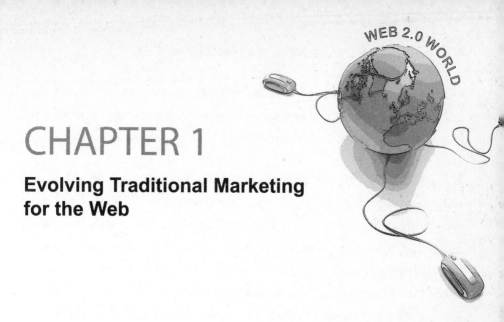

CHAPTER 1

Evolving Traditional Marketing for the Web

"If you do not change direction, you may end up where you are heading."

\- Lao Tzu, philosopher and the father of Taoism

Start Slow with Web 2.0 and Social Media

There is a common scene playing out in offices across the country. The owner, CEO, or whoever runs the show calls the person in charge of marketing into their office for a talk. While each discussion varies slightly, the gist is the same. The boss tells the marketing person they need to go "**Web 2.0.**" When asked for clarification, the boss will inevitably cite an article they read on a plane about how companies need to have a Web 2.0 presence. They will typically mention a competitor that is ahead of the game. While the conversation usually ends there, further interrogation would likely reveal the boss is not 100 percent sure what Web 2.0 even means.

While this scenario is an oversimplification, there are far too many companies jumping in to the Web 2.0 arena without the proper planning they would put in to any other marketing initiative. There is a pervasive feeling that simply being there — joining social networking sites or starting a blog — will yield amazing results. In fact, the opposite is true. While a poorly executed print advertising campaign will simply result in little or no conversions, a poorly planned and executed interactive campaign may result in a backlash. Think the Internet version of a public relations fiasco.

It is important to treat a Web 2.0 marketing campaign as you would any other campaign, with sufficient planning, attention to detail during execution, and analysis during and after the fact. That being said, traditional marketing principles were not written with the Internet in mind and require interpretation in order to apply to Web 2.0 marketing. There are also some rules specific to the interactive medium. It is important to understand these marketing principles, both old and new, before taking your company to the next level online.

Which Principles to Apply to Web 2.0 Marketing

There are three main principles anchoring every basic marketing textbook that translate very well to interactive marketing. Those include the five P's of marketing, marketing myopia, and relationship marketing. It is important to fully understand what they are, how they apply to traditional marketing, and how they can be adapted to the online world.

Five P's of marketing

Depending on when you took your last marketing class, you may only be familiar with the four P's of marketing, also referred to as the **marketing mix**. Originally coined by Michigan State University marketing professor E. Jerome McCarthy in 1960, the four P's include:

- **Product**
- **Price**
- **Place**
- **Promotion**

Many marketing experts widely accept the addition of a fifth P on the list, which is especially relevant to interactive Web 2.0 mediums like social networks:

• **People**

There are several variations of the concept, including an assertion by B.H. Booms and M.J. Bitner in their 1981 book *Marketing Strategies and Organizational Structures for Service Firms* that there are in fact seven P's in the marketing mix. There have been additional P's suggested for inclusion in the marketing mix since McCarthy's time, including packaging, public opinion, political power, people, process, and physical evidence. The most common addition, and most relevant to Web 2.0, is people. Both models are widely accepted standards that can be applied well to Web 2.0 marketing, though the fifth P (people) is particularly relevant in interactive marketing.

Product — The physical product or service, including packaging, warranty, etc.

Price — Accounts for profit margins, competitor pricing.

People — Customer service, appearance, attitude

Place(ment) — Distribution channels, market coverage, logistics.

Promotion — Communication and selling through advertising, PR, etc.

Fig. 1: The 5 P's of traditional marketing, also known as the marketing mix, are important pieces of any marketing effort.

While individual elements in the overall marketing mix, the five P's overlap one another considerably. As illustrated in Figure 1, making a strategic change to a single element will have an impact on the others. For example, positioning your product as a luxury brand in high-end boutiques will invariably impact the promotional tactics, brand image, and the price point itself.

Product

Product refers to the actual good or service being marketed. This includes specific elements like packaging, warranties, and support, which can affect the customer's perceived value of the product or service. This is an area where Web 2.0 can make a significant impact. The Internet affords companies new ways to provide support for their customers through services like FAQ pages, archived manuals, and easy access to contact information. Web 2.0 takes this even further with support mechanisms including online chat, forums, and even customer-driven support.

When a customer has a complaint or question about your product, he or she now has more resources than ever to look for assistance. Instead of calling your office or visiting a retailer, many turn to search engines and discussion forums for help. Realizing you are not in control of the conversation about your company can be very frightening. While negative comments are inevitable, loyal customers are normally quick to come to the defense of a quality brand. One option is to participate in these forums, answering questions and soliciting feedback. Another option is to provide a forum on your own site where customers can interact with other customers as well as your support staff.

Price

The second P in the marketing mix is price, which deals not just with the dollar amount you assign to the product but also to its position alongside the competition. Price takes in to account the cost to produce the product and the margins, and the customers will dictate what they are willing pay. The quality of the product and the support services provided alongside it determine a product's final price.

There are additional factors to consider for companies that are able to sell their product or service online. For example, a wholesaler may offer a product directly to the consumer through its website, reducing certain expenses. Without the retailer's markup to consider, a lower cost may be offered. Or a company can find ways to reduce the cost of interacting with their retailers by moving processes online, allowing them to reduce their wholesale price.

Place(ment)

The third P is place or placement. This deals not only with the physical location that a product is available to customers, like boutiques or big-box retailers, but also the product's position in the market. The distribution channel itself comes in play with a product's placement. The marketing for a product can vary depending on the places it is sold as well as the specific demographic it is intended to target.

Identical products are often marketed very different based on their placement as it relates to different demographics. A great example is pregnancy tests. There are two distinct buying groups for this product: people trying to get pregnant and those trying to avoid it. While the product inside the box is the same, the placement of these products is very different. One version of the product might be located near contraceptives, while the other might be placed near feminine or even baby products. This example shows how the different P's are inter-related, as the placement of a product can actually dictate the price a customer is willing to pay for it.

The Internet has opened up several options for small businesses in regard to placement and distribution. Marketers must decide how to sell their product online, whether directly to the consumer or through a network of retailers. Once again, this relates directly back to the price and the value of the product itself. Placement takes on another meaning in a Web 2.0 world. Small businesses need to consider not only the place where the product is purchased, but also the place their product has in their customers' lives.

Promotion

Marketing and advertising are often confused, though advertising is represented in one of the five P's in the marketing mix. Promotion, the fourth P in the marketing mix, deals with all activities designed to increase awareness of the product. These may include advertising, public relations, direct sales, and even branding. Another element of promotion is word of mouth. The Internet, specifically social networking sites, has made this an even more important factor in the marketing process, not only through encouraging happy customers to tell their story but also quickly identifying and solving customer complaints.

When bringing a new product to market, small businesses must now consider the buzz, if any, the product will generate. An interactive demo or strong review can be a catalyst for a wave of discussion before a product is ever released. This can be seen every time Apple is scheduled to release a new product like the iPad or when Microsoft makes an update to the Windows® operating system, with bloggers and even news outlets caught up with speculation about features, leaked pictures and reviews, and rumors about prices. While small businesses cannot expect that type of media circus when releasing a product or service, generating a buzz, even a small, local one, is a great way to use the community for promotion.

People

The last of the five P's is people. People evolved as an extension of product, which includes things like support and now community. However, people does not just refer to those outside your company but also the influencers within your organization that impact the product. People like Bill Gates, Steve Jobs, or Richard Branson are as much a part of their brands as the products themselves. Consider how a bad experience with a cashier affects your perception of the store as a whole or how an overly helpful waiter makes you rave to your friends about a restaurant. People are intertwined with brands and products for better or worse. Your job is to make sure the people within your organization are strong brand ambassadors.

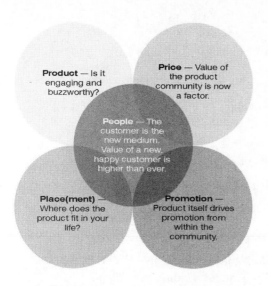

Product — Is it engaging and buzzworthy?

Price — Value of the product community is now a factor.

People — The customer is the new medium. Value of a new, happy customer is higher than ever.

Place(ment) — Where does the product fit in your life?

Promotion — Product itself drives promotion from within the community.

Fig. 2: The 5 P's translate well from traditional marketing to Web 2.0 and social media marketing.

Web 2.0 has expanded the relationship your employees have with your customers. Most Facebook users list their employer in their profile, as do many on LinkedIn, MySpace, Twitter, and other sites. An employee's actions can affect your brand long after he or she leaves for the day. This makes education and guidelines for your staff critical in controlling the message coming from your company.

You can see in Figure 2 how the meaning of each of the five P's has been tailored to fit into Web 2.0 marketing. The Internet is simply a new medium to promote, support, and sell your company's product or service. While some have tried to expand beyond the four or five P's, author Lon Safko (**www.lonsafko.com**) instead created a new list of five P's, illustrated in Figure 3. They are specific to **social media**, a broad term that describes websites or tools primarily made up of user-generated content that foster interaction among users. While social media strategies, including each one covered below, will be examined in greater detail in subsequent chapters, Safko's list is relevant to the evolution of traditional marketing principles to Web 2.0 marketing. The list includes:

- **Profiles**
- **Propagate**
- **Produce**
- **Participate**
- **Progress**

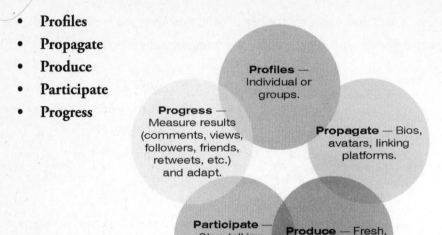

Fig. 3: Unlike the traditional five P's in the marketing mix, the P's of social media are cyclical.

Profiles

The first P is a reference to the profiles you create both as an individual and for your company on various social networking websites. The profile is a very important tool that can dictate how often your page is accessed. Most users will come across your page through a profile search based on your location, industry, product, or other keywords. Therefore, writing a strong profile rich in keywords will help users find your page when searching for people or companies related to your products. *Chapter 6 will outline the specific steps a company should take to create a strong profile.*

Propagate

A page with no content — more specifically, no fresh content — is worthless. Once a user sees little or dated content on your page, they will go straight to the next result from their search engine; this is a missed interaction with a potential customer. Propagating your pages with fresh, relevant content will not only inform and engage users, but will also lead to greater exposure in the search engines. This can be as simple as uploading photos, creating links to blog posts or other articles you have written, or even linking to relevant pages on your website.

Produce

The third P, produce, takes propagate a step further. While it is important to leverage the existing content you have already created for other campaigns, it is key to create content specifically for each medium. Each social networking platform has a distinct set of users that expect you to follow the standards set forth by the community. Posts on Twitter, for example, are limited to 140 characters. Just repeating a longer status update from Facebook or a post from your blog may result in several words being clipped off. You should instead write a post that is truncated to fit within the site's parameters. Tailoring your content for each medium is a great way to win the trust and acceptance of others on the platform.

Participate

Participation is imperative in the world of social networking. More important still is the right type of participation. Social networkers expect interaction, not advertising. Simply using these forums as a new place to post your daily specials or white papers, or technical or marketing-focused product research documents, is akin to walking into a mixer and shouting your elevator pitch. You will be ignored or even ostracized. This is why some social networks enforce strict rules about how companies can partake, like Facebook. According to the Internet marketing blog Marketing Pilgrim (**www.marketingpilgrim.com**), Facebook prohibits businesses from creating individual profiles; instead, they must create "pages." Participation goes beyond simply posting content and should include asking questions, answering others' questions, and building relationships.

Progress

Measuring the success of a social media marketing campaign is not a simple task but is a crucial step that must be taken. Indicators like hits, friends, comments, and views must be analyzed next to your campaign's goals. While a dollar amount cannot be assigned to how many followers you have on Twitter, there are tools to track whether those followers turned in to customers from clicking on a link you posted to your account. Measuring progress will help you focus your efforts where you have the most chance for success, as well as helping you support your decisions to the boss. *How to measure your progress will be detailed in Chapter 11.*

CASE STUDY: SELF-MONITORING MESSAGE BOARDS IN ACTION

Sue Koehler, marketing and customer service team
Monterey Boats
(www.montereyboats.com)

The pleasure-boating industry, while offering a high-tech product, has been notoriously low-tech when it came to marketing. Monterey Boats, a manufacturer of luxury boats ranging from 18-foot sport boats to 40-foot cruisers, decided to take a huge step forward by creating a customer portal on its website. Inside, Monterey owners could order parts, browse manuals, and, most importantly, interact with other owners through a message board. While the Williston, Florida, company was excited about the new platform and the potential cost savings in their support department, they were admittedly concerned about the inevitable issue of dealing with angry customers.

Monterey had two choices: Moderate each comment before it went on to the board, or let users post in real-time but risk negative or offensive comments making their way on to the site. Monterey decided to start with the moderated approach, knowing they could move to the other method based on the feedback. The only potential drawback of this decision was users would not see their posts immediately and may become disenfranchised; however, Monterey dedicated Sue Koehler, a member of the company's marketing team, to make the board her first priority.

The discussion board started to build users, with owners showing off pictures of their boats and sharing their favorite places to visit. About a week after the site went live, the first negative comment came in. The comment was related to a technical detail of the user's boat, and Monterey decided to approve the comment and quickly post a response addressing the concerns. What happened next surprised everyone involved with the project:

"Before I even had a chance to write a response, our other owners came to Monterey's defense," Koehler said. "They chastised the member for his tone and even helped solve his problem."

Monterey decided to let other similar posts go to the board and saw the same results. The community actually began to police itself.

"Not only did users help each other out with problems, but they also came to the defense of the brand when owners of a competitor's boat would post a comment," Koehler said. "We found the board had more credibility when responses came from other owners rather than the company, so we ended up taking a more passive approach."

The site grew to more than 10,000 active members and requires little moderation, with Koehler still handling that task on her own.

"We don't need to lead the conversation, but instead just need to be there participate," she said.

Marketing Myopia

For the better part of the 19th century, as well as the first quarter of the 20th century, trains were the most efficient way to travel. For a fraction of the time it would take to head West in your covered wagon, you could travel from one end of the country to the other in relative comfort. The train companies were not short on power or money as a result of this transportation monopoly. Despite that fact, trains gave way to automobiles, which eventually led to passenger air travel. Even though the demand for passenger and freight services were on the rise, the once-giant train companies were left dead in their tracks.

Looking back, the train companies missed out on a major opportunity. They looked at themselves as companies that provided access just to trains as opposed to the broader service: transportation. They should have expanded their own offerings by investing in emerging technologies like automobiles and aircraft, rather then hope the new technologies would not catch on. This is exactly what Theodore Levitt was referring to when he wrote about the concept of **marketing myopia** in 1960 in the Harvard Business Review: "The vision of most businesses is too constricted by the narrow understanding of what business they are in." In a purely literal sense, myopia is an ocular term to describe shortsightedness. Levitt however used myopia to refer to the lack of foresight businesses often suffer from.

Examples are not hard to find today — just look at the music industry. Some 50 years ago, the record labels' business was clear: They sold songs. The medium evolved from records to 8-tracks to cassettes to CDs, but the basic principle stayed true: If you were an artist and wanted to sell your music, the record companies had the only proven vehicle to market your work. When MP3s hit the market, the proliferation of file sharing via the Internet changed things completely. There are scores of examples of unsigned and self-promoted musicians finding success through tools like Apple iTunes® music application.

So, record companies are being forced to rethink their model. Where they once sold songs, they must now focus on selling entertainment. Bands have become brands. According to the *Guardian,* major labels are turning to executives with product marketing backgrounds to help open up new revenue streams from their artists to offset the dip in CD sales. There may be a time very soon when music is free and record companies make all their profit from concerts, T-shirts, and licensing.

Newspapers are shrinking every day, both in terms of their staff and the number of pages they print. At the same time, many are reinvesting in a richer online presence. Oil companies are putting more effort in exploring alternative energy sources. In 20 years, we will not just have newspapers or oil companies; we will have information and energy providers. Every industry eventually evolves, and only those companies with a broad vision and the willingness to adapt will survive.

The theory of marketing myopia can be used to not only look at your business as a whole, but also look differently at how you market it. Think back to promotion and placement from the five P's of marketing. There is a good chance your company is promoting your product with its blinders on. You should consider more than just what promotional strategies have worked in the past; you must also consider what new approaches you can employ moving forward. This can lead to both a new audience and a cost savings over traditional promotional methods.

The same holds true for placement. The record companies allowed Apple iTunes to grow to the force it has become in the market by only placing their products in conventional music stores. Now iTunes has tremendous power when it comes to setting the price point for the entire industry. Some newspaper companies have taken notice of the shift in consumer's information consumption habits, as illustrated in Figure 4, before it is too late. Not only have they embraced the Internet as a new place to post content and sell ad space, but they are also starting to branch off to new technologies like e-readers, which download subscribed content to a handheld device; this is a great step for the publishers. Just imagine how much they would save in ink, paper, delivery, labor, and office space if all newspapers were read digitally.

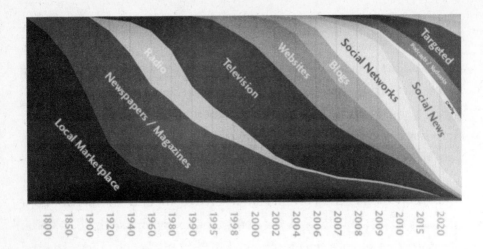

Fig. 4: Where is everyone? Author Thomas Baekdal shows how information sharing has and is evolving on Baekdal.com (**www.baekdal.com/articles/ Management/market-of-information**).

While it is important for companies to identify and move to new channels for distribution and promotion, it is also important to approach these changes with a fresh outlook. Newspapers are reproducing content online, but they have also changed the way they publish. In the past, reporters turned in their stories at the end of the day in time to be printed in the next morning's edition. Luckily, they have not taken this process to the Internet. Readers expect different types of information from the two sources, and they expect to hear the latest news as it happens, even if it is after hours. The website should offer the latest information and breaking news, while the print edition serves as a more in-depth recap of the previous day's stories with additional commentary. It is important to look at all aspects of your company as your marketing evolves. New placement options may require a different pricing model, as is the case with iTunes. Likewise, different promotional tools may call for a change in the product itself. Therefore, it is essential to step back and look at the full impact of each decision you make.

It is a good idea to keep an eye on what your competition is up to. At the same time, you should avoid following too closely in their footsteps, even if they have had great success. There are countless examples of "social media success stories," and it is easy to fall in the trap of repeating the same process. While you should glean elements of their methods, you need to find ways to evolve the idea and make it your own. Remember, you are dealing with a vocal collection of consumers online, and a copycat campaign, especially one in the same industry, will be seen for what it is. Users expect, and are more willing to embrace, new and innovative ideas. So think twice before trying to turn someone else's success story in to your own.

CASE STUDY: TWITTER-GENERATED SALES IN ACTION

Robbie Vitrano, chief branding and design officer
NakedPizza (www.nakedpizza.biz)

The big pizza chains are notorious for their traditional marketing tactics, including door hangers, coupons, and — of course — an endless stream of television commercials. They are also known for their historically unhealthy food. Louisiana-based NakedPizza is looking to change that perception.

Founded in 2006 in an area hit hard by Hurricane Katrina, NakedPizza's goal was to use an established comfort food to spread a message of wellness and healthy living. "We're borrowing 95 percent of Papa John's and Domino's operational DNA, using it like a Trojan horse to introduce a great-tasting, nutritionally correct pizza, wrapped in a social mission and powered by a scalable, disciplined business model," said Robbie Vitrano, NakedPizza's chief branding and design officer. "NakedPizza hacked pizza to make an unhealthy and popular fast food healthy."

While the pizza may be the Trojan horse, Twitter is the platform helping people find it. With more than 7,000 followers just one year since joining Twitter in early 2009, the restaurant has extended its message beyond its serviceable area of New Orleans. But that is fine with Vitrano, who points out that NakedPizza is "actually more a social media company that happens to sell pizza."

"In making an unhealthy and popular fast food healthy, we're able to raise consciousness about nutrition, health and the food supply, as well as the social impact and obligations of a modern, profitable business," he said. "Twitter turbocharged our ability to tell our story, hear from people and interact."

Twitter also charged sales. Since joining the social network, the company boasts 15 percent of sales directly from Twitter. The company, which includes a Twitter button on its point of sale system to track return on investment, expects online ordering to make up 40 percent of its business for 2010.

Twitter has led to more than just orders. NakedPizza set up a franchising company in September 2009 and already has contracts to develop stores in several new markets. While the product is driving followers to the company's Twitter account, it is the content that is turning those followers into sales. NakedPizza has found the perfect balance of sales and promotional messages with educational tweets to keep users engaged.

"It's still about an authentic connection," Vitrano said. "Treating social media as one to many platforms is wrong, be you local or global. It's about communication and reciprocity. You need to provide value in the form of information or offers."

Relationship Marketing

The concept of connecting directly with your customers is not new — just the technology is. For decades, most marketing has focused on advertising and promotions. The one obvious exception, and precursor to the social marketing influx, is **relationship marketing**. This principle is centered on the concept that it costs much more to earn a new client then it does to keep an existing one happy. In fact, a study by ChannelCorp

Management Consultants Inc. suggest the sales and marketing cost of retaining an existing client is about 14 percent of the sale price, while new client acquisition may be as high as 95 percent on the initial sale. Couple that with the power of a referral from a happy client, and you have a great marketing strategy. The only problem is that relationship marketing, at least traditionally, is expensive.

A primetime television spot will get you in front of millions of people, though not all of them are necessarily in your target audience or paying attention — some are probably asleep. But running a television ad is a much easier way to reach the masses than a one-on-one interaction. Think about the prospect of connecting personally with your customers before the Internet age. It starts with the in-person sales meeting and continues well after the sale with details like customer service surveys and support phone calls. Granted, these things taper off the longer you retain a client because they will inevitably become more familiar with your product and processes. Regardless, these things are expensive. There is staff, training, office space, communication infrastructure — the list goes on, but study after study has shown the value of building relationships.

The increase in profit is the result of several factors, identified by R. Buchanan and C. Gilles in their article "Value managed relationship: The key to customer retention and profitability" from the *European Management Journal:*

- The cost of acquisition occurs only at the beginning of a relationship, so the longer the relationship, the lower the amortized cost.

- Long-term customers tend to be less inclined to switch and tend to be less price-sensitive. This can result in stable unit-sales volume and increases in dollar-sales volume.

- Long-term customers tend to initiate free word-of-mouth promotions and referrals.

- Long-term customers are more likely to purchase ancillary products and high margin supplemental products.

- Regular customers tend to be less expensive to service because they are familiar with the process, require less product education, and are consistent in their order placement.

It does not take a big shift to see results, either. In fact, according to Frederick Reichheld and W. Earl Sasser Jr.'s article "Zero Defections: Quality Comes to Services" from the *Harvard Business Review,* just a 5 percent rise in customer retention can result in a 25–85 percent bump in profitability. Those kinds of numbers make the investment well worth the cost. Social media marketing has drastically reduced the obstacles, more specifically costs, to attaining those kinds of numbers. A well-planned interactive campaign can put you in front of your customers and cost nothing but your time.

The value of relationship marketing has not evolved over time but rather the tools available to small businesses have seen a shift. Just take Facebook, for example. It is one of the best ways for companies to build one-to-one relationships with clients. Here is a look at just how far its reach extends, according to Facebook's statistics page as of April 2010:

- More than 400 million active users
- 35 million users update their "status" every day
- 50 percent of active users access Facebook every day
- The average user spends more than 55 minutes on Facebook per day

Not only does Facebook have the volume in terms of the number of users, but it also has their attention at the rate of almost an hour every day. While those numbers are staggering, keep in mind Facebook is only one of several successful social networking platforms, and depending on your company's target demographic, you may elect to be on one or several networks. Thousands of businesses have seen the power and reach of sites like Facebook. In fact, there are more than 1.6 million active "pages" on Facebook. (A page refers to a profile for a business, nonprofit, or other organization.) Of that number, 700,000 belong to local businesses, such as coffee shops and boutiques that only serve their neighboring community. The average user becomes a fan of two pages per month. However, the most important number is the cost to create those pages: zero. What would have cost tens of thousands of dollars just a decade ago now only costs time.

Twitter, a micro-blogging service, has seen exponential growth over 2008 and 2009, though its overall users still lag behind Facebook. *Learn about Twitter in more detail in Chapter 8.* At Twitter's first official Chirp conference in mid-April, cofounder Biz Stone revealed the site has more than 100 million users and is growing at a rate of 300,000 per day. Twitter users are especially attractive to small business marketers, not just for their numbers but for how they use the system. Many access Twitter via mobile devices, allowing for interaction at the point of sale. However, some of the most successful uses of Twitter have been in the field of customer service and support.

One of the best examples of great support through Twitter comes from Southwest Airlines. While not a small business by any stretch, Southwest's approach is a model for just about every other company, and can easily be scaled. Figure 5 shows a snapshot of Southwest's Twitter page from Dec. 7, 2009:

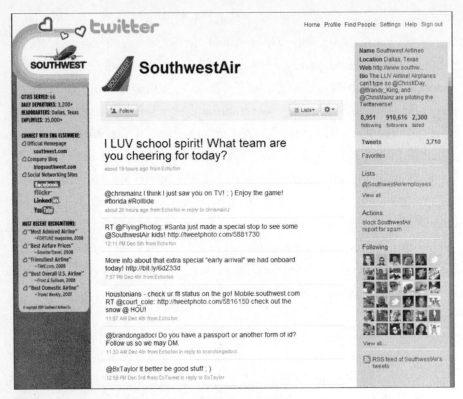

Fig. 5: A peek at Southwest Airlines' Twitter page.

Just from looking at this page alone, there are several great things to point out. First, take a look at the profile information in the upper right of the page. Transparency is important on social networks since customers would much rather connect with people than companies. Southwest accomplishes this by introducing the specific people responsible for managing the corporate account. Then, a look at Southwest's number of followers — people subscribed to receive their tweets (individual posts) — shows a strong fan base. Finally, the number of tweets as of December 2009, which is more than 3,700, is a good indicator that Southwest is an active participant online.

Looking at the left side of the page also shows some great information. Twitter allows users to upload a custom background image, and Southwest has taken advantage of this by including links to other ways to connect with the airline. Southwest marketers remembered that not everyone is comfortable connecting through every medium on the Web. If a user comes across a particular tweet, a posting on Twitter, he or she can elect to reach out to the company using the other options given on the page.

The most important aspect of Southwest's relationship approach is evident in the main body of the page. It is important to notice the frequency of tweets, but the most important thing is the type of conversation that is taking place. Notice Southwest is not using Twitter as a platform to simply promote specials. While some of that does take place on their page, the vast majority of its tweets are in response to other users' comments, both positive and negative, about the airline. While the chapter on social networking will delve deeper into the topic, you can see any of the tweets that use the @ symbol are referencing another user.

Southwest is also connecting with users on Twitter in a language they are used to. While you would expect a business letter to have a professional tone, Twitter users, as well as people on most social networks, are used to a more conversational tone. Much like texts or instant messages, Tweeters use acronyms and other abbreviations to get their thoughts across in as few characters as possible. Just look at the first tweet from Southwest, where they use "luv" instead of "love." **Emoticons**, textual representations of facial expressions, are also commonplace.

For every good Twitter example, there are several companies not using the tool to their full potential. While it is a much larger airline than Southwest, Delta has a much smaller social networking presence. In the later half of 2009, most of its tweets focused on announcing promotions and other company news. However, since the beginning of 2010, Delta has significantly ramped up its Twitter activity. As a result, Delta has more than doubled its followers from around 17,000 in the middle of January 2010 to more than 45,000 as of April 2010. The number of its total tweets went from 63 to more than 700 during this same period, a testament to the heightened focus on Twitter as a relationship-management tool. Figure 6 shows a recent snapshot of Delta's page, including many instances of one-to-one customer interaction.

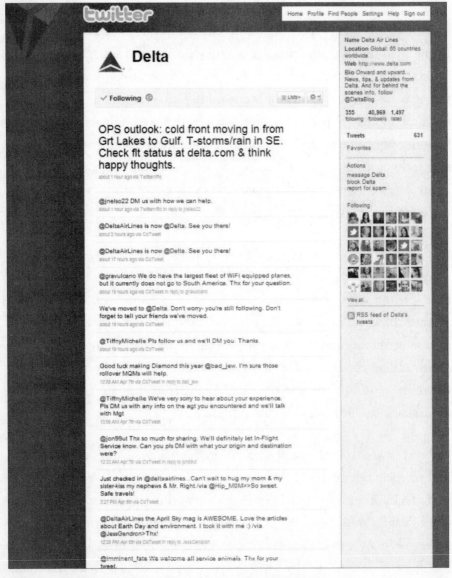

Fig. 6: The Delta Airlines' Twitter page on Apr. 8, 2010.

Right away, you will notice the difference in the number of followers. Southwest passed 1 million followers as of April 2010, but Delta only had about 4 percent of that. That could be because of an enormous gap of more than six months in activity on Delta's part, as shown in Figure 7. Before that, Delta only tweeted 30 times in the two years its account was active. In Delta's defense, their

> With heavy holiday travel volume, please make sure to give yourself plenty of time if headed to the airport today. #Delta
> 9:53 AM Dec 23rd, 2009 from web
>
> Waivers for NE, Midwest flights affected by winter storms. Get the latest updates> http://bit.ly/Delta_Advisory
> 3:24 PM Dec 22nd, 2009 from web
>
> Winter weather certainly doesn't make holiday travel any easier. Check your flight status & stay tuned for tips, updates, and info. #Delta
> 3:03 PM Dec 22nd, 2009 from web
>
> What a day! Celebrating 80 years of nonstop service today. Pass the cake! More on Delta's history http://bit.ly/4k46l
> 10:23 PM Jun 17th, 2009 from web
>
> @DavidArchie - glad you like the video! We like yours too. Vote for fav onboard snacks here http://tinyurl.com/n9sqgs. Have a great flight!
> 2:28 PM Jun 11th, 2009 from web
>
> mixing up some yummy drinks for passengers. Try 'Summer Sizzle': 1 part Disaronno Amaretto, 1 part Stirrings Apple Martini Mix, stir & serve
> 9:56 AM May 15th, 2007 from web

Fig. 7: Delta Airlines Twitter page shows a significant gap in its tweets in fall 2009.

business model is very different than that of Southwest, which caters to a different type of audience. However, that does not excuse the approach Delta has taken with its tweets. Before Delta's radio silence, very few of its tweets were in response to other users; however, even those were directed at celebrities, such as singer David Archuleta, and not customers with a specific comment or complaint.

This goes back to the point of playing by the rules of the platforms you are on. Delta would have been better served to simply reserve its username and post a tweet asking users to visit its website for support. By putting a presence on Twitter beyond that, customers expect a certain level of service, which Delta was not meeting in fall 2009. A search for comments referencing Delta from other users in late December 2009 showed a plethora of opportunities for Delta to either remedy a customer service situation or weigh in while potential customers are choosing which airline to use. Some of the comments were complaints about baggage fees, while others commented on weather delays. Another still was asking for opinions on which airline was better among Delta, United, and American. However, all of these comments went unanswered — by Delta, at least. The real issue was that other Twitter users who were following those who wrote the comments would reply and add commentary (known as **retweeting**), thus sharing the same comments with their followers. In a matter of minutes, one comment seen by 100 people could morph into one comment seen by 1,000 people. That is how a simple situation can quickly turn into a full-blown public relations nightmare.

Delta has since taken control of this, and the results are evident. Customers are now offered resolutions for their issues and are able to truly connect with the brand. Delta is now turning customers into brand ambassadors.

While the comments are not going to magically become positive just because you are monitoring them, it does give you a chance to make things right. A more recent search for people talking about Delta in April 2010 showed a significant difference. Rather than talking just about the brand, people were talking to it, referencing @Delta in their posts. That is because they know Delta is listening and will respond. Posts included one asking for a representative to contact him about a concern, while others were questions about baggage limits or simply praise for good service.

One final thing to remember on the topic of relationship marketing is that the customer is in control of relationship terms. You need to be flexible and ready to interact with your customers wherever they choose, be it on Facebook, LinkedIn, Twitter, or the next social networking platform that is sure to pop up soon. You can only truly build a solid relationship by listening to your customers and addressing them.

KEY TAKEAWAYS

✓	Do not start a Web 2.0 campaign without a plan of attack.
✓	Consider how your decisions on one aspect of your marketing plan affect the other elements of the 5 P's.
✓	Take a step back and look at where your company fits in the market-place. Do not let yourself get bogged down with labels about your company or industry.
✓	Relationships can have a huge impact on the bottom line, but only if you listen.
✓	Get ready to change with your customers.

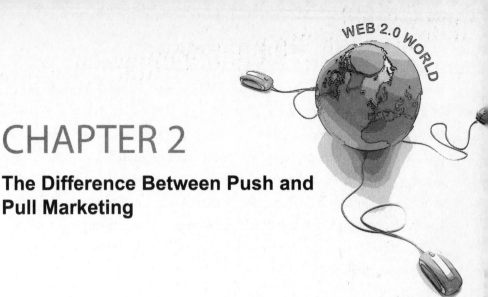

CHAPTER 2

The Difference Between Push and Pull Marketing

"There cannot be greater rudeness than to interrupt another in the current of his discourse."

- John Locke, English physician and philosopher

The shift in power from promotional strategies like television and print advertising toward Web 2.0 campaigns is clear, but it is important to understand the reasons this is happening. First of all, the emergence of Web 2.0 tools as a way to digest news, information, and entertainment has eaten away at traditional media's stranglehold on the market. But it is much more than just the presence of these new tools that has led to their importance. What we are witnessing is not as simple as the evolution from radio to television in the 1950s; both of those platforms provide users with content that is sprinkled with advertising. The advancement to Web 2.0 is a complete paradigm shift in the way consumers interact with brands.

What is Push (Outbound) Marketing?

For over a century now, the model has been the same: Advertising provides and breaks up the content. This includes commercials during radio and television shows, advertisements in magazine and newspaper articles, and most recently, banner ads on websites. While some of these have seen more success than others, you are almost always looking at very low conversion rates, often fractions of 1 percent, and the Direct Marketing Association puts average conversion rates for direct mail at under 3 percent. These avenues have no consideration for where someone is in the purchasing process. The automakers continue to show you new car commercials even if you just bought a new car. **Push marketing** is not and can never be personal. The one constant about push marketing is its focus on interruptions, and nobody likes to be interrupted.

When you tune in to watch a show, you are interrupted at least four times an hour with a few minutes of commercials each time. (In fact, hour-long shows average around 42 minutes of actual show with the remaining 18 minutes left for commercials and promotions.) When you flip to the next page of a magazine to finish an article, you usually are interrupted by a full-page (or at least half-page) advertisement. And when you click on a link to an article you want to read, you often have to click "close" to get rid of the overbearing ad that is covering the content you really want. That is push-or-interruption marketing, and it is pretty evident why it is not very effective. Advertisers only used it because there were not any other options.

One-sided conversations

The fundamental flaw with push marketing is the fact that it is a one-way discussion, not a conversation, as illustrated in Figure 8. Businesses are pushing their message out to the masses; some may be potential customers, but many probably are not. And of those potential customers, not all are listening. This does not give any feedback options to the consumer, nor does it allow for personalization of the message from the advertiser. In a time before social networking, this was fine — not perfect, but fine. But when your customers are connected to one another as they are in social networks, only the company is outside the communication loop in a push-marketing scenario. This is still acceptable, but only if your product is perfect. Once there is even the slightest customer service issue, being out of the loop goes from inconvenient to downright dangerous.

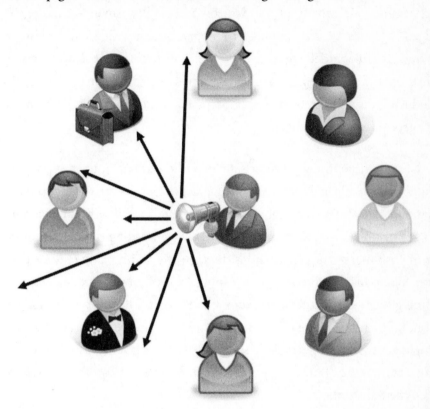

Fig. 8: Traditional push marketing is directed at people who may or may not be listening and may or may not be in your target demographic.

At the same time new communication platforms have inched toward the mainstream, new technologies have provided consumers with better tools to block interruption marketing. The result is an even lower conversion rate. One example is the digital video recorder, DVR, which gives viewers the ability to fast-forward through commercials on previously recorded programs. Advertisers have responded by integrating the commercials in to the programming by way of strategic product placement, the result of which is yet to be fully measured. The buzz around shows like NBC's 30 Rock writing things like Cisco's teleconferencing platform into their scripts is a testament to its effectiveness. When asked if he likes Cisco's TelePre-cense technology, Alec Baldwin's character goes so far as saying, "Of course. It continues to be the gold standard by which all business technology is judged." He even directly quotes the company's tagline, "Cisco, the human network." Cisco added the clip to its website (**http://videolounge.cisco.com**) soon after it aired. Though this particular instance created a signifi-cant buzz for the product, this may become a less effective tactic when the joke gets old with customers.

At the same time, the growth of satellite radio has cut in to the profits of long-established broadcast stations. The fact that users are willing to pay a premium to avoid advertising — the majority of satellite radio program-ming is commercial-free — is a clear statement regarding the public's opin-ion of push marketing. The trend is the same even with relatively new plat-forms like e-mail marketing. The combination of government regulations defining what constitutes spam and smarter filters has forced companies to modify their mass-mailing strategies. More passive strategies like the bought ads from Google that are shown to users within the Gmail interface is a great example of how advertisers are finding new, less-intrusive ways to reach their customers.

Another factor impacting traditional push platforms is the sheer number of options available when it comes to taking in information and enter-tainment. In the past, television was a great advertising tool specifically because of its ability to put your message out to an enormous audience. While the numbers are still significant, DVRs are not the only thing affect-ing the medium. More savvy viewers are electing to watch their favorite shows online on their own schedule through sites like Hulu (**www.hulu.com**). The online versions typically do not include the same advertisers as in the broadcast versions and instead use banner ads or shorter commercial breaks. Others prefer to watch complete, advertisement-free seasons on DVD — something Netflix has made relatively inexpensive. While the producers still make money, the advertisers are cut out of the mix. The same holds true for magazines, radio, and especially newspapers, which are now competing with citizen journalists using blogs to get information out to the masses.

What is Pull (Inbound) Marketing?

If interruptions are the problem, then pull marketing is the solution. The pull philosophy started as a supply chain issue that evolved into a marketing concept. In terms of logistics, the pull approach addressed a problem with product development where a product was brought to market with no real impact from the consumer and therefore no real understanding of the actual demand for the product. The pull concept relies on customers' driving innovation. This may include only manufacturing products after an order has been placed. The side effects include a longer lead time and higher production cost, but it is one way to ensure a satisfied customer.

Pull marketing also hinges on the customer driving the process, as illustrated in Figure 9. Where outbound marketing is a one-way process, inbound marketing is based around the concept of letting your customers know where you are; this allows them to find you when they are ready to make a purchase. Properly positioning your company both online through search engines, blogs, and webinars, and offline through speaking engagements, published articles, and networking, you establish yourself and your company as thought leaders, or experts, in your industry. Doing these things will keep your company on top of mind, as well as on top of the search results. In short, you will be there for your customers when they are ready to buy.

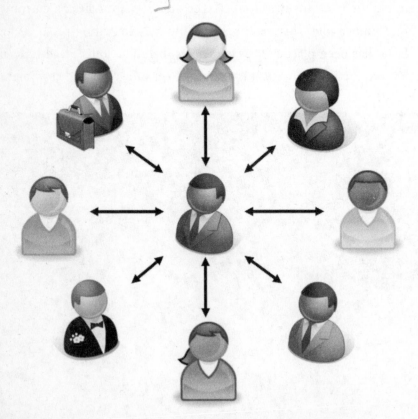

Fig. 9: The pull marketing approach encourages interaction with your prospects on their terms.

The Only Way to Market on a Budget

If you have learned one thing from this book so far, it should be that traditional and outbound marketing is expensive. As a small business, you need an approach that combines the maximum reach and effectiveness with the minimum cost, both on your budget and your time. Inbound marketing is the answer. Just look at the costs associated with just a few of the main tools used in inbound marketing, the specifics of which will be explained thoroughly in the following chapters.

Search engines

When customers are ready to buy, they will often turn to the search engines. While they may already be familiar with the product they are looking for, they want to look for deals or new providers they were not previously aware of. Nearly 95 percent of clicks to go the first 20 results for a given search, so getting your company to the top of the list, or at least on the first page, can have an enormous impact on your leads or sales. The best part: It does not cost much, if anything, to get there. That said, there are companies ready to charge you thousands of dollars to do the very things described in this book. Your best weapon is knowledge. Knowing what factors the search engines use to rank sites is the key. But know too that the search engines are always changing the rules. The search engines are notorious for modifying their ranking criteria as companies find gray areas around the rules.

Most of your investment in search marketing comes down to time. First off, you need to make sure your website's page titles are optimized. Next, you will want to update your meta-data, identifiers within your site's HTML code used to describe different areas of your site. Search engines look at the site's code, not the graphical front-end users see. Therefore, arranging your code to put keyword rich elements higher is also important. *This will be discussed in detail in Chapter 5.*

Another key element in determining your rankings is the number of inbound links your site has. In a way, links are votes for your site. But unlike an election, these votes are looked at not only for their quantity, but also their quality. A link from a major site is worth several links from lesser-known sources. Links are one area where some companies do invest money, paying for placement on sites with strong search rankings. These links can cost anywhere from around $100 a month to well more than $1,000, depending on the site's credibility.

A less-expensive way to achieve the same goal is to provide a reciprocal link to someone in order for him or her to link to you. Just make sure to be selective, as too many links can have an inverse effect on your rankings. Google recommends you keep the number of links per page under 100, excluding internal links, like those to other pages within your site. Longer pages like sitemaps can get away with more, while short pages should come in well below that figure. For example, a page with just a few paragraphs of text should have fewer than 25 links, so the search engines do not see a discrepancy in the ratio of content-to-links that might indicate foul play.

The next step is optimizing your content. This can be the most time-consuming portion. A high ranking is contingent on not just relevant, keyword-laden content but also on fresh, up-to-date content. Every time a search engine analyzes, or "spiders," your site, it takes note of any changes. New content tells the spider your site may be more important than sites with older information on the same topic.

Blogs

One of the best ways to push fresh content to your website is through a **blog**. Couple this with the fact that many blog engines are free, and you have a great resource for the small business marketer and a great place to focus much of your effort. A blog is a much stronger tool when it lives under your company's main domain name because all of the blog's content is seen as content on your site. Internal blogs require some investment in hosting and possibly programming. *You will learn how to do more of this in Chapter 6.* However, an external free blog, such as WordPress or TypePad, can still have an impact on your site's inbound links.

In addition to the search engine impact of a blog, it can also help you build a community of followers, furthering your goal of thought leadership. Offering tips and news about your industry through your blog will make you a go-to source for prospects researching your industry, including those that may be potential clients, as well as reporters covering it. Take Beth's Blog at **www.beth.typepad.com**, for example. The blog, which covers social media use for nonprofits, ranks in the top 50 on the *AdAge* Power 150 blog rankings. In addition to being a resource in her industry, Beth Kanter is also the CEO of Zoetica, a company providing consulting services to nonprofits. Kanter keeps the blog as a resource and not a sales pitch, and she recognizes that in the end, customers will remember your expertise and may choose to work with you over a company they do not have a similar relationship with.

Webinars

Webinars, a term used to describe Web-based seminars, are another great inbound marketing tool to also promote thought leadership while also introducing you to new prospects. If you put out a message by mass e-mail or on your blog talking about a special you are having on a new product, you may see a bump in sales, albeit a small one. However, if you put a message out to the same channels about a free webinar on emerging trends in your industry, chances are you will see a much higher response. Conversion rates are generally low for e-mail marketing, but something offering value at no cost has a better chance of making it to your audience.

While these are not sales, they are leads. Each of your webinar's attendees represents someone with a serious interest in your industry. By avoiding a direct sales pitch during the presentation, you are working on building a relationship with your audience. And, as with blogs, customers will remember your knowledge and willingness to share it when it comes time for them to make a purchase.

Social networks

This is where things really get interesting. **Social networks** have provided small businesses with a forum to interact directly with customers and potential buyers. Unlike running a focus group or public surveys where you are limited to the number of people you either pay or talk with, social networks let you get feedback from a pool of millions, and the price cannot be beat. There is no cost to set up a page on Facebook, an account in Twitter, or a profile on LinkedIn, a popular business-networking site that is great for B2B relationships. With all of these tools, the primary cost once again comes down to time. However, unlike blogs or webinars, which do not offer any shortcuts, third-party applications within social networks let you automate portions of the process. After setting up your profiles and accounts, your blog can be set up to push content to your LinkedIn page, your Twitter feed can update your Facebook status, and so on.

The importance of social networking to a small business is not just in your communication with customers, but also in monitoring conversations among customers about your brand. Setting up alerts or specific searches is also free and will let you know instantly when users discuss your company.

Do not pay for exposure: Produce it

One of the similarities among all of the examples you have just read is the focus on producing your own content. Traditional outbound marketing requires significant budgets to push your message to an audience. At the same time, it is impossible to know whether you reached your target audience and if they were even paying attention. Mediums like newspaper ads, television and radio spots, and billboards require your target to be paying attention at a particular moment, which is something you cannot guarantee.

Inbound marketing takes the opposite approach. By producing your content and making it available through archived webinars, blog posts, bylines, and on social networks, you are leaving the information for your prospects to find when they are actually looking for it. And when they find it, they will perceive it differently from how they would if you put the same message in a television ad. Rather than interrupting your prospects, you are actually providing them with important information in your articles, webinars, and blog posts. This information presents you as a partner, not just a vendor.

CASE STUDY: EFFECTIVE PULL MARKETING IN ACTION

Shel Horowitz, author of Grassroots Marketing and coauthor of Guerilla Marketing Goes Green
www.frugalmarketing.com

Shel Horowitz knows a thing or two about inbound marketing. In fact, he has been either writing about it, speaking about it, or doing it for nearly 30 years. Horowitz has written eight books about everything from *Grassroots Marketing for Authors and Publishers* to his latest book, *Guerrilla Marketing Goes Green: Winning Strategies to Improve Your Profits and Your Planet.*

In addition to his writing, Horowitz is also a marketing strategist and copywriter for hire. He employs pull-marketing techniques almost exclusively to promote himself to potential clients. Some of the strategies he has used include social media marketing and his website. At the same time, Horowitz notes that pull marketing is not a new strategy exclusive to Web 2.0. He has been using inbound marketing to acquire coverage in traditional media outlets, publish articles, and conduct speaking engagements for the past three decades. He has seen his efforts pay off time and time again, with these pull-marketing efforts turning complete strangers into customers.

"One of my current clients, working with me to go from unpublished writer to published author, clipped a story out of the local newspaper about me and filed it for several years, until she was ready," Horowitz said. "Another current client was referred to me by an industry expert who knows me through a longstanding social media PR campaign."

His public relations efforts land him between 30 and 60 interviews a year, many of which result in free publicity. He has been covered in the *New York Times,* the *Boston Globe,* and *Fortune Small Business,* as well as more than 250 radio stations.

"In fact, I can't really think of any marketing I'm doing that isn't a pull medium, other than business cards and the occasional trade-show flier," Horowitz said.

Comparing the Costs of the Two Approaches

In addition to the other benefits of pull marketing, cost savings ranks among the highest with small businesses. Where push marketing costs real money to produce and place advertisements, pull marketing, after some initial investments in infrastructure, costs primarily your time, although there may be some costs setting up your blog, depending on which approach you take. From there you are looking at a few hours each month to write your posts. Most Webinar platforms charge either a low monthly fee or a cost per session; however, hosting the archived video of the Webinar indefinitely is free through several online services. *This will be discussed in detail in Chapter 9.*

Making sure your inbound marketing strategy has the same reach as an outbound campaign requires a well-executed **search engine optimization (SEO)** strategy. However, it is the very act of producing your content that can have the greatest impact on your rankings. Again, after some initial investment to optimize your website's code structure, it is just a matter of maintenance and fresh content. At the end of the day, inbound marketing will cost you less out of pocket and provide you with more qualified leads and better customer relationships. Web 2.0 technologies have leveled the playing field with the heavy hitters in your industry. Now, it is up to you to take advantage of the tools available to you.

KEY TAKEAWAYS

✓	Push (outbound) marketing is an interruption-based approach to a mass audience.
✓	Pull (inbound) marketing puts your company in a position where your prospects can find you when they are looking for you.
✓	Tools like webinars and blog posts cost less to produce than push methods and elevate your status as a thought leader in your industry.

CHAPTER 3

Making Your Website Truly Interactive

"No one will improve your lot if you do not yourself."

- Bertolt Brecht, German poet and playwright

Early websites were an extension of push marketing, consisting of the equivalent of an online billboard. For inbound marketing to be effective, there needs to be a consistent call to action across all your messages. With your message scattered across blogs posts, in online videos, and on various social networking sites, your website needs to act like a hub. Every one of your other efforts should drive visitors to the heart of your Web 2.0 marketing campaign. While many of the other Web 2.0 tools like social networks and online videos are hosted externally, giving you restricted control over the look and feel, your website is the one place where you have complete control of the users' experience.

There was nothing inherently wrong with Web 1.0 sites. Companies at the time were restricted with the technologies and tools available to create a great online experience. The results were informational sites giving users little more than an online brochure with a contact form. Other sites went further to actually let visitors buy products, though the process was not always smooth for the customer in the beginning. Much like outbound marketing, Web 1.0 was a shotgun approach pushing one-way messages. The goal was simply to present your marketing message to whoever came to your site.

However, the goal of your website has changed. With Web 2.0, the goal is to turn people into customers. Simply sharing your message needs to be replaced with cultivating relationships. The main concept of Web 2.0 is to facilitate interactive experiences, and your visitors expect that on your site. You have brought them there through interactive tools like social networks and blogs, so the rich experience of those external tools needs to carry through to your site.

Using Interactive Elements

Adding interactivity to your site is a broad and overused term, almost as broad as Web 2.0. Getting back to the theme from Chapter 1, it is important to make sure you choose the right interactive elements for your goals. Adding new technologies merely because they are popular will not have the same effect as adding a feature that ties in closely with your business model. That luster will wear off quickly unless the feature actually adds value to your site. Think back to when the Adobe® Flash® platform was introduced to websites. Flash allowed developers to create animations that could integrate video and sound effects that were commonly used as introductions before a user saw the regular website. They quickly went from cool presentations everyone ogled to a speed bump standing between your customer and the information they were looking for. Today, users cannot find the "skip" button fast enough. Many more are likely hitting the back button instead. Here are just a few of the more common interactive features that savvy Web users have come to expect from a great website.

Content management systems

Adding or updating your website's content used to be a job akin to adding an addition to your house; you had to get the site's builder involved. There were estimates, timelines, and — most importantly — there were costs. The alternative of attempting to do it yourself was equally daunting. First you needed to download the latest version of the site from the server. Then, you either dusted off your HTML notes or tried to wade through the Microsoft FrontPage® website program or Macromedia (now Adobe) Dreamweaver® application to make the edits before using FTP (File Transfer Protocol) to update the server. Trying to fix one thing often broke something else on the site, leading to broken links, missing images, and ultimately bringing the developer in again.

Content management systems (CMS) are great tools that allow a website's administrator to make all the updates they want to without needing a computer science degree. A CMS lets you add, edit, or delete content in select areas of any page on the website with no knowledge of HTML or other coding languages. This is typically the main body area that holds the content. Not only is a CMS an easier way to update a site, but it can also provide some peace of mind. One wrong keystroke while editing your site's HTML code could result in anything from broken images to pages not loading at all. CMS tools eliminate the need to edit the site's code for simple content changes. Some tools even allow administrators to create new pages altogether. Rather than using HTML code or complicated programs, most CMS systems include a WYSIWYG (what you see is what you get) editor, as in Figure 10, laid out much like most word processors. This means no Web development experience is necessary to make these types of changes.

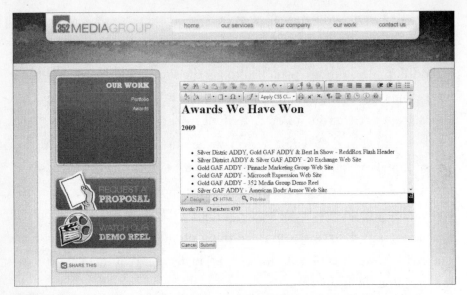

Fig. 10: A WYSIWYG editor on the 352 Media Group website lets users insert links and images as well as edit text right on the page.

Though commercial CMS products have been around since the mid 1990s, developers were slow to push the tools, and it is no surprise why: Giving customers the ability to make their own updates meant less work for them. But building a new site now without a CMS is like buying a car without power windows. It looks the same from the outside but is an unnecessary pain that can easily be avoided.

There are several different types of CMS available, ranging from free plug-ins to enterprise solutions that can cost tens of thousands of dollars. Small businesses with a typical website should budget between $2,000 and $5,000 for a CMS, which typically includes the license and installation on your site. Here are some features to look for in a strong CMS:

- WYSIWYG editor

- HTML editor for more complex changes

- Support for **cascading style sheet** (CSS) classes, which ensure the design elements of the site are maintained (font styles, text sizes, colors, and other parameters for different categories of content)

- Ability to rollback changes to a previous version

- Ability to create new pages from existing templates

- Ability to link to files (documents, videos) you upload

Some of the free CMS options include Movable Type, Drupal, and OpenCMS. Enterprise-level solutions like Ektron or Microsoft Office SharePoint are a better choice for sites with more complex or custom features since they offer more customization and configuration options. Telerik's RadEditor for ASP.NET AJAX, which licenses for $999 and would require about that much for professional installation on your site, is a good middle ground that provides all the features needed for most sites.

There are other points to consider, depending on who will be updating your site. For example, many tools give you multiple levels of administrator access, meaning a lower-level employee's changes are not made live until approved by the main administrator. A live demo is the best way to ensure the features you need are included, so make sure you test-drive any system before putting it to use on your site.

Once your new CMS is up and running, it is important to use it. Do more than simply updating outdated information, although that is what you should focus on. You should take advantage of the tool to add more keyword-rich pages about the products and services you offer. This fresh content will score big points with the search engines, resulting in higher rankings under related search terms. Remember that having a CMS is not an alternative to building your own site; it is just a difference in the foundation on which the site is built.

CASE STUDY: EFFECTIVE YET LOW-COST TOOLS IN ACTION

Geri Stengel, president
Ventureneer (www.ventureneer.com)

Websites today need to stay current in order to hold a visitor's attention, not to mention that of the search engines. That is why a good content management system is such an important element of a successful website. In their infancy, CMS tools were expensive and therefore almost exclusively used on high-end custom websites. The open source programming community has responded with several free tools for small business, including the popular Drupal platform.

Geri Stengel is president of Ventureneer, a consulting company that offers online education and peer support service for small business making a social impact, including nonprofits. The company's site evolved from Stengel's personal blog in to a complex corporate website including multiple membership access levels, file sharing, forums, and a full search, among other tools. The site is built on the Drupal platform, which boasts users from individuals all the way up to The White House (**www. whitehouse.gov**). Stengel admits that the CMS system is not without its flaws, especially when it comes to the WYSIWYG editor.

"While uploading content is easy, what you see isn't always what you always get," she said. "Line spacing and bullets frequently need fine-tuning. This can be time consuming."

She has also experienced compatibility issues across different Web browsers, an all-too-common problem even professional Web developers must constantly wrestle with. "There are also incompatibility issues with Macs," she said. "Some functionality such as indicating content falls if multiple categories on a drop menu isn't available on a Mac."

While Drupal is a feature-rich tool, Stengel feels it does not completely eliminate the need for a professional developer's help. "A skilled programmer is needed for the branding and much of the functionality we require," she said. "These costs add up and can be tens of thousands of dollars."

At the end of the day, the little things are worth it to Stengel and Ventureneer. They have a website they are proud of that they can update with relative ease. And when compared to commercial programs, Stengel said, "In all honesty, I don't find free software any more buggy."

Forums

Forums were one of the first interactive elements to become commonplace on companies' websites. A direct descendent of early bulletin board systems (BBS), online discussion forums are tools that let visitors post questions or comments that can be commented on by other users, including your company's employees. Forums can be used presale to let potential customers interact with current customers, reading reviews or other posts about your products. Forums are also common after the sale to provide customer service support or simply to create a community with other customers who share similar interests. Forums, also referred to as discussion boards, can vary in cost from free tools like MyBB to more feature-rich components like Telligent that can cost a few thousand dollars. These options come with varying degrees of customization, with the more expensive tools seamlessly integrated into your site's design.

There are several configuration options to consider when adding a discussion forum to your site, the most important of which is moderation. As you learned from the Monterey Boats Case Study in Chapter 1, you can elect to allow any comments be live instantly on your site or have each go through a moderator for approval before posting to your site. While the former leaves you open to more risk, open forums are typically more active and tend to police themselves. A good strategy is to start with an open policy and modify it if you start to see abuse. Most forum tools capture the IP address, a digital signature that identifies the computer or service provider of the author, which allows you to ban users that do not adhere to the rules of the forum. Requiring users to create an account that confirms their e-mail address before posting is another way to moderate a forum by removing offending contributors, although this still is not foolproof.

Newsletters and e-mail promotions

Despite the bad rap spammers have been given, **e-mail newsletters** are still a great way to interact with your customers or leads. A good newsletter and e-mail marketing strategy can keep your company on the top of your current customers' minds and bring in new customers. The most important element of a successful e-mail strategy starts with your list. While many companies promise to sell or rent lists within your target demographic, the best list is always a homegrown one. People who have specifically asked to receive information from you are obviously more likely to act on those messages.

Therefore, the first step is to integrate a "subscribe" feature in your website. This can be done as part of an existing contact form, during an e-commerce checkout process, or as a standalone form on any page of your site like the example in Figure 11. By piggybacking the newsletter subscription to other interactions on your site, you can quickly grow a strong list that has more value than a purchased list ten times as large.

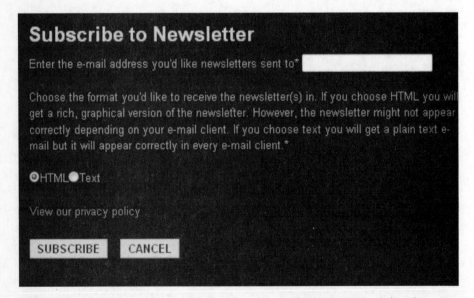

Fig. 11: A sample e-mail subscription form that allows users to select how they would prefer to receive e-mails.

A basic newsletter feature can cost as little as about $2,000 to install — some companies just charge for installation and others make you pay per e-mail sent — and can be used in a variety of ways to interact with your customers. Some examples include:

- Weekly/monthly newsletter with company announcements, product information, or industry news

- Invitations to webinars, other online events, or offline events like trade shows

- Announcements for coupon codes, specials, or new product notifications

More advanced newsletter programs can take the experience even further, especially in regards to e-commerce sites. Some second-tier features of more robust newsletter programs may include:

- Automatic reminders to reorder a product based on the date of the last order (helpful for items like cosmetics or food products whose supply only lasts for a certain period)

- Coupons to users that have abandoned their shopping cart enticing them to complete their order

- Suggestive selling by offering products related to others ordered in the past

Regardless of how you use a newsletter tool, it is important to monitor its success. Most tools let site owners see at least some information, like that shown in Figure 12, about how many e-mails went out, how many bounced back, the number that were opened, whether links within the e-mail were clicked, and if users unsubscribed from the list as a result of that e-mail. These statistics will help in determining the best time to send different types of e-mails in the future.

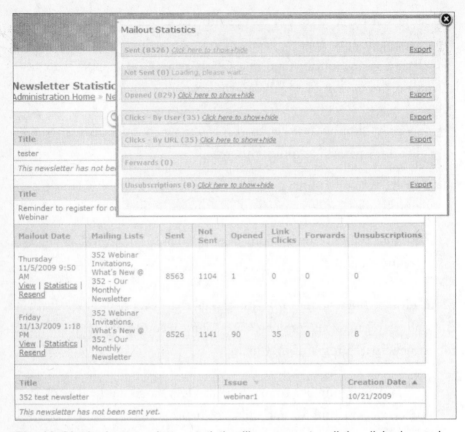

Fig. 12: Monitoring newsletter statistics like open rates, links clicked, unsubscribes, and messages forwarded will help improve future campaigns, as shown in this example from 352 Media Group.

CASE STUDY:
FREE NEWSLETTERS FOR
MARKETING IN ACTION

Dallon Christensen, creative director
and founder
FirstStep Concepts
(www.firststepconcepts.com)

Dallon Christensen is the creative director and founder of FirstStep Concepts, a business that helps other companies gather and evaluate data about everything from cash flow forecasting to market research. As a small business owner himself, Christensen appreciates the need to market his company on a budget.

He is no stranger to using free online tools to market his business; in fact, his website is created on the WordPress platform. He also takes advantage of social networks to stay in contact with his customers and leads.

Christensen wanted to take that customer interaction one step further by adding a newsletter tool to his website. After comparing custom programmed solutions, fee-based software, and free services, he settled on MailChimp (**www.mailchimp.com**). The website offers subscription services from $30 a month for mailing lists up to 2,500 users, all the way to $690 per month for lists up to 150,000 people. As a new business, FirstStep Concepts was able to take advantage of MailChimp's "Forever Free Plan," which allows them to store up to 500 e-mail addresses and send 3,000 e-mails per month at no cost.

The tool gives FirstStep Concepts all of the functionality they need. "MailChimp provides me with an excellent and free interface for people to subscribe to my newsletter," Christensen said. "I can customize the colors on the subscription form to make it integrate with my website."

Of course, there are tradeoffs by opting for a free tool. For example, even with the design customization choices Christensen mentioned, integrating a plug-in does not always work perfectly. Integrating the subscribe box without an HTML or CSS coder's help may have undesirable side effects, either on the subscribe tool itself or even on other elements of the site. FirstStep Concepts' widget, for example, does not wrap the text on the heading, shown in Figure 13, a problem seen on several other sites that use the tool.

MailChimp is also a completely self-serve program, which, if you have never used an e-mail marketing provider in the past, might be a daunting task. They provide plenty of resources like training videos and webinars to help customers get up to speed, and even have approved partner relationships with what they call "MailChimp experts."

But for FirstStep Concepts, the potential drawbacks are worth the cost savings. And they are not alone. According to the WordPress website, fewer than 23,000 users have installed the plug-in on their blog platform alone as of March 2010.

Christensen is a believer in free online marketing tools. "I am beginning two research campaigns for future classes using Google Apps," he said. "I use the Apps service for my e-mail, and I will link separate Google forms to my website. I will be able to have visitors link to my forms and provide me with valuable information for future class offerings."

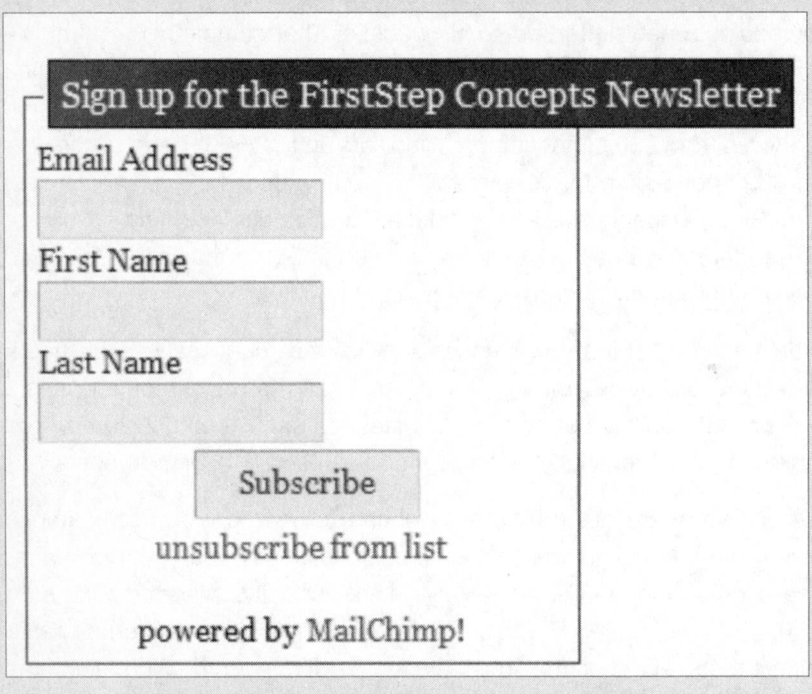

Sign up for the FirstStep Concepts Newsletter

Email Address

First Name

Last Name

Subscribe

unsubscribe from list

powered by MailChimp!

Fig 13: MailChimp's subscribe box stretches beyond the right edge of the widget, likely due to an issue with text wrapping.

Polls/surveys

Polls are one of the quickest ways to solicit feedback from your site's visitors. Not only do they encourage users to interact with the website, but they also provide immediate feedback on their answer by showing the results of the poll so far. Polls, like the example in Figure 14, can be about anything related to opinions about industry news to feedback on the website itself. Free plug-ins (tools) are available that provide a few lines of code that you can paste, or embed, in your CMS's HTML editor. The tradeoff here is they will not maintain the design elements of the page. Customizable

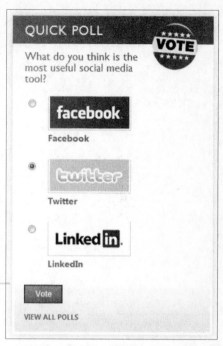

Fig. 14: A poll question engages users by encouraging them to interact with your site.

polls typically cost less than $2,000 to design and integrate on a website, and include a robust backend administrative area to add new questions and manage results.

Surveys act in much the same way but offer even more insight. Expect lower response rates on surveys than polls due to the time they can take to complete. Many sites will offer an incentive such as a coupon or raffle entry to encourage more users to respond, though that may skew the results. Most survey tools let you select between multiple choice (with single or multiple answers accepted), true or false, or short answer responses for your questions. More complex systems even allow for contingent questions, such as "If yes, then..." scenarios.

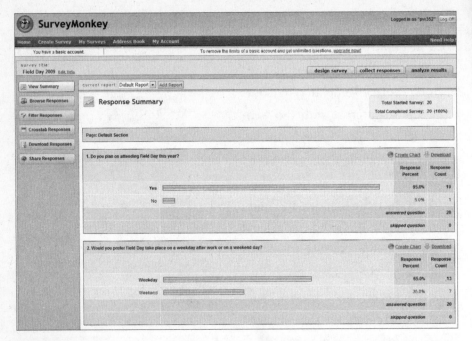

Fig. 15: Surveymonkey.com offers a free survey-generator tool with a strong reporting feature.

There are several free survey tools available online. SurveyMonkey (**www.surverymonkey.com**) as shown in Figure 15, is one of the most popular, letting users create a free account with the bare essentials: 15 different types of questions like multiple choice and short answer, with 10 total questions for each survey, and a choice of preset design themes. For a monthly fee, users receive more options both in the design of the surveys and the reporting elements, including charts, data exports, and response filters. However, the surveys still require leaving your site. Integrating a custom survey feature into your own site costs anywhere from a few thousand dollars to $10,000 to install. The cost may be worthwhile if this is a feature you intend to use regularly or if you need customizations like very specific reports or a unique user interface. Otherwise, this is one component where the free or monthly charge options normally suffice.

Contact forms

Contact forms are other early Web 2.0 tools that allow site owners to collect information from users. They have evolved over the years from simple form fields, drop downs, and radio buttons (like the form in Figure 16) to include more customization. For example, a contact form today can show different questions based on earlier responses and allow users to upload documents or images as part of their response. While they can be used for a variety of tasks, most contact forms allow users to ask questions or request a proposal from the business' site. Forms are typically sent to the company via e-mail but can also be stored in a database to facilitate data dissection.

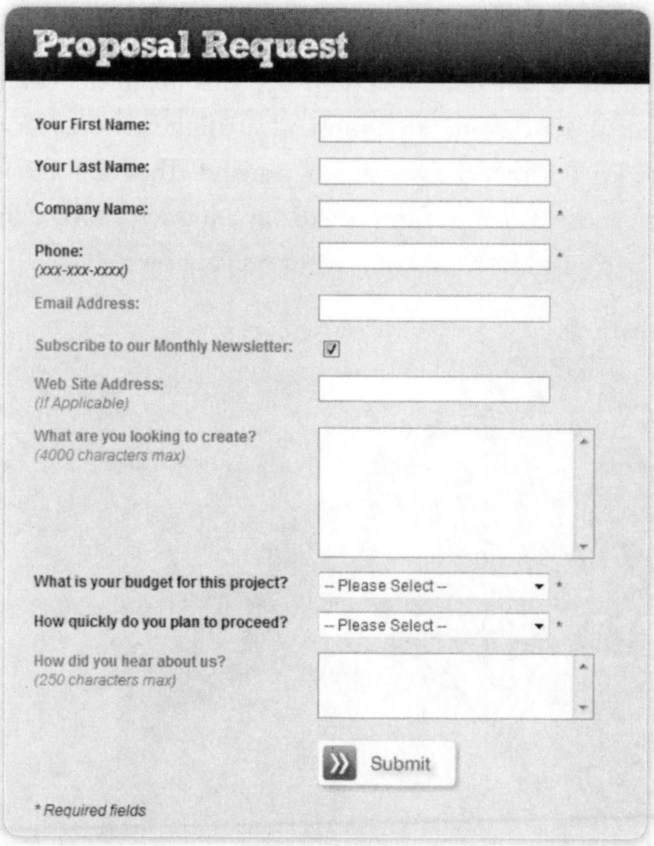

Fig. 16: A simple contact form, like the one shown from 352 Media Group, can include both required and optional fields.

Low-cost Ways to Implement and Maintain These Elements

Similar to the inbound marketing strategies described in the last chapter, much of the work on your website can be done for free using the tools available online. However, the result, while feature-rich, may end up looking like a patchwork quilt. Adding components from different partners at different times, it is easy to overlook your brand image. Remember: Your website is the nucleus for all your Web 2.0 marketing efforts, so it is important that the professional image you have created on your blog, in webinars, and on Internet videos is carried through to your site. At the same time, many free services are only free because they have their own contextual advertising built in, usually through text ads on the side of the page, banner ads, or the occasional pop-up. This might not sound overly intrusive at first, but consider that most advertising networks serve up ads based on the keywords of the website they are on. These ads are outside of your control, and can change from day to day. Nothing is worse than inadvertently seeing an ad for your competitor on your own site.

With that in mind, you should identify the handful of features that are most important and relevant for your site. Consider what your audience is most likely to use, as well as what lines up best with your business. For example, an e-commerce site should have a newsletter to keep in contact with past customers and encourage repeat business — a feature not as important to a company using its site to acquire new leads. The elements you may need for your website is specific to your company. Those critical features should be integrated in your site to maintain a consistent brand image across your various online marketing efforts. Other less-crucial features can be added as budget permits, with free tools being integrated as necessary. You do not want to use too many free tools because even though many give you some design leeway, few will seamlessly integrate with the website's appearance. It is best to invest in the must-have features for your clients, and save the free tools for those features that are not your site's main focus.

Targeted landing pages

Many small businesses develop their website around the premise that visitors enter only through your homepage. However, this is rarely the case. While in a brick-and-mortar store you can control the entry point, the same cannot be said for the Web. Different pages on your site will earn rankings based on the keywords on that page, so when users search for those terms, they are linked to that specific page. It is imperative that your website's navigation be consistent across all pages, so users can quickly get where you want them to go.

Multiple entry points could be conceived as a liability, with so many entrances difficult to manage. For example, retail stores know exactly where a customer will enter their store and can put specific products in specific locations based on that. What would happen if customers could beam themselves right in the middle of a store? Positioning product placement could be a real problem because you would not know where people would be entering. However, different entry points online can also present an opportunity. By analyzing your website's traffic through tools like Google Analytics shown in Figure 17, you can identify where and how different user groups find your site and tailor the experience to those groups through **landing pages**, which refers to the page through which a user enters your site. While the next chapter will cover how to earn high rankings for those pages, it is also important to understand the value of targeting your site to key demographics.

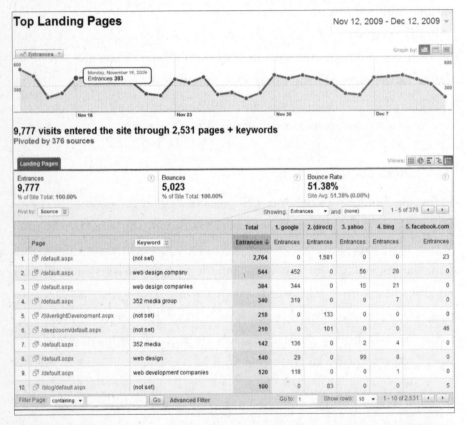

Fig. 17: A sample Google Analytics traffic report from 352 Media Group shows what pages users entered through and the keywords they used to get there.

Take a restaurant's website, for example. While the main focus of the site may be to attract new diners, the restaurant may also have a catering business. Since the main goal of the site is to push users to make a reservation, it may be difficult for catering customers to find the information they need. You can address this concern by creating and optimizing a page specifically for catering. When a user enters through this page from a search for "restaurant catering," they will see a more specific call to action, whether it is to download a catering menu or more often to complete a contact form requesting a consultation. Take a hard look at your site's analytics to identify possible groups based on the keywords searched, pages visited, and the percentage of visitors who are turning in to leads and customers. *This will be covered in depth in Chapter 11.*

While the other navigation should still be available in case a user found this page by accident, focusing the body content of a page on the specific audience and the corresponding call to action can have a big impact on your conversion rates. Some search engine experts go so far as to encourage you to remove all other navigation from your landing pages, but this is a problem for two reasons. First, as much as you would like to control how a user finds you, there are no guarantees that the person coming to that page is really in that audience, and the non-targeted users should not be neglected because they happened upon that page. Second, a page with no navigation stands less chance of earning high search engine rankings. As you will learn in the next chapter, pages are ranked based on a variety of factors, with links to and from other popular pages, including those within your own site, weighing highly on that list. Do not exclude the other navigation; instead, make sure that it is not the visual focus on the landing page's design. You do not want to let it get in the way of the goal and take customers away from your call to action.

Creating a compelling call to action

Once you get a user to your website, which is no small feat, you need to convert them into a lead. This is where a compelling call to action comes in. This is the hook that catches your visitor's eye and encourages them to take the next step toward becoming a customer. From your perspective, the goal is having a user either purchase a product or complete a contact form to request more information. To the visitors, the goal is getting a great deal or other valuable information. A simple "contact us for more information" is rarely enough to convince the visitor to part with their personal information.

When creating your call to action, remember that your visitors' goal is not the same as yours. They did not wake up this morning with a burning desire to give you their money. You need to show them the value, and after years of being blasted on infomercials, "while supplies last" just does not create the sense of urgency that it used to. Rather than focusing on pushing a purchase, consider using the other Web 2.0 tools you have already created as a lure. "Download our latest webinar" is a great call to action, as long as you capture their contact information before making the content available. The same can be said for white papers, e-books, or even trial offers. The customer is getting information they are obviously interested in without a commitment, and you are getting the contact information of a motivated buyer. And if you have done your webinar well, your prospect is hearing about the virtues of the type of products or services you offer. At the end of the experience, you should come across as an industry expert — an industry expert with a new lead.

You should test different calls to action to see what is most effective. Experiment with different wording or different incentives. By tracking your visitor-to-lead conversions, you can create an effective call to action for each of your landing pages.

KEY TAKEAWAYS

✓	Your website is the center of your Web 2.0 marketing efforts.
✓	Integrate tools that encourage interaction with your customers.
✓	Not every user finds your site the same way. Use landing pages to increase conversions from different user groups.
✓	Create compelling calls to action to turn visitors into leads.

CHAPTER 4

Getting Search Engines to Notice Your Site

"The ultimate search engine would basically understand everything in the world, and it would always give you the right thing. And we're a long, long ways from that."

- Larry Page, Google cofounder

You have your website. Your landing pages are ready to go, each with a great call to action, and you have oodles of interactive features. Now it is just a matter of getting people there. Social networks are great. So is word of mouth, and even a small dose of offline marketing. But nothing will have a bigger impact on your site's traffic, ergo your bottom line, than making nice with the search engines.

As a small business, chances are you lack the "household name" factor that many large companies rely on to drive traffic to their websites. Instead of going online to look for your specific company, your prospects are likely doing a Web search to find you based on your product or service. Without the budget to earn national brand recognition, search engine marketing becomes the most critical piece of your marketing pie.

For companies that rely on traffic from the search engines, a drop of just a few spots in the search results for key terms can have an exponential effect on leads. In 2006, AOL inadvertently released very specific, very private data about what people were searching for, which included addresses, social security numbers, phone numbers, and even things that would be considered criminal activity, according to the Internet technology blog Tech-Crunch (**www.techcrunch.com**). While this put AOL in a tight situation, it also gave insight to just how important a ranking is. This data was quickly analyzed, and the SEO software firm Axandra (**www.axandra.com**) found that in more than 20 million searches from 658,000 subscribers, 47 percent clicked on the first result in the search engine, while just more than 12 percent clicked on the second. Jump ahead to No. 5 on the list, and only 5 percent clicked through. Being first in the results means your site should expect four times more traffic than a competitor just one spot lower.

There is more to it than just getting good rankings in any search engine. Being ranked in the right search engine can make all the difference. According to the online researcher comScore's September 2009 report, Google has a strong hold on the market, with a 65 percent share. Yahoo.com ranks second with 19 percent, while Microsoft's Bing.com, the Ask Network, and AOL combine for roughly 16 percent. That is based on more than 13.8 billion total searches in that period. Based on those numbers, it stands to reason that you should optimize your site based on Google's Webmaster Tools recommendations. However, keeping an eye on the changing market share is also a good idea. Be aware of any anomalies in your industry. For example, e-commerce websites may want to pay more attention to Bing and Yahoo, both of which offer popular product search tools.

Pay Per Click Versus Organic

There are two different ways to appear on the search engine results for a given keyword. The first is an **organic ranking**, which is based on several factors determined by each engine to provide the most relevant content for a particular search query. The second are paid results, where companies bid in an auction-style system for placement on certain results. The paid model is generally **pay per click**, where the company is only charged if their link is clicked. You can see each option in Figure 18.

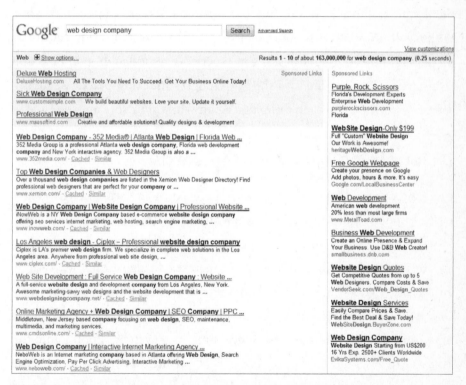

Fig. 18: A search on Google in December 2009 showing paid results on the top and along the right, with organic results in the main body area.

Long-term savings versus initial cost

Organic rankings have no direct cost, and search engine visitors consider them to be more trustworthy than pay-per-click rankings. That explains why 70 percent of users click on organic results, while only 30 percent click on the paid ads, according to search engine marketing firm Enquiro (**www. enquiro.com**). However, organic rankings can take considerable time to kick in. Bringing a new site online does not mean it will show up in search results right away. And when it does, changes you make may take weeks or even months to impact your rankings. As your site builds more steam, it will be spidered more often, but that does not help bring in traffic right away. That is why small businesses should take a balanced approach at first using paid search, which starts as soon as you make a payment, to supplement your traffic as you wait for your organic results to catch up. As your rankings improve, you should taper off your paid search terms and focus on maintaining your rankings. If you experience a sudden drop in rank due to a change on your site or a shift in Google's indexing practices, simply start up your pay-per-click campaign again while your sort out the issue.

Determining Your Best Keywords

In a perfect world, your site would be indexed by the search engines and ranked under all the appropriate **keywords** important to you — interestingly enough, that is actually the goal of the search engines, and why they are constantly tweaking and retweaking their search algorithms, the formulas they use to determine the order of their results. However, your competitors are likely stacking the deck in their favor by flooding their sites with keywords, forcing you to do the same. Some may even be slipping into the ethical gray area between optimizing their website and trying to trick the search engines to improve their search engine clout. That is why you need to optimize your site to achieve the best rankings you can while still making sure you stay within the guidelines set forth by the search engines, the importance of which will be evident by the end of this chapter. So here are a few tips for determining which keywords to focus on in your site.

1. Understanding how your customers search for you

Despite everything you have just read, there are situations where a No. 1 ranking for a search term is useless, specifically when no one is searching for that term. In order to create a good search strategy, you need to put yourself in your buyers' shoes. While you are all-too familiar with the technical terminology surrounding your product, your client may not know those words. Clients may search based on their need rather than the name of the solution. For example, they do not know they need your "Portable Weather Station Deluxe 2000"; instead, they may search for a "portable digital thermometer barometer combo," meaning you should optimize for that keyword phrase as well. Understanding how your customers think is a vital step to finding the right keywords.

2. Geographic targeting for local businesses

Not all businesses serve a national, or even regional, audience, and at the same time, not all customers want to work with someone across the country. That is why it is important to remember to include regional keywords. If your barbershop serves only the Kansas City area, then a website visitor from Omaha is not that important to you. Also, it is much easier to earn a top ranking for a more specific keyword. As of December 2009, "barber shop" returns 12.5 million results on Bing, while a more specific search for "barber shop Kansas City, MO" brings up only 750,000 results, as shown in Figure 19. While that still sounds like a huge number, and it is, the first five results are the Local Listings, Bing's (**www. bing.com**) version of the Yellow Pages. Remember, most people do not make it past the first page, much less the first few results, so optimize for your city, region, and even your state by including those keywords in your site's content, headings, and code.

Fig. 19: Many search engines show a different type of result for searches that include a location.

Even if you are not restricted to a geographic area, you can still use area-specific keywords. For example, create a landing page for each state that highlights the work you have done for customers in those areas. Identify the major markets where you have had success in the past, and create pages for those cities. It will take more time, but as the statistics bear out, having ten No. 5 rankings on city-specific terms should have more value than one No. 50 ranking on more general terms.

3. Identifying buy words versus other search traffic

Just as targeting by location can be an effective strategy, so to can focusing on surfers at different stages in the buying process. Take mattresses, for example. If your store sells mattresses, you would rather be ranked high under a term like "serta perfect sleeper euro top mattress" than simply "mattresses." While the latter is likely searched more often, the former is a clear buying sign. Someone searching for a specific brand and model of a mattress has likely done his or her homework and is now looking for the best place to make a purchase. A search for "mattresses" might be a potential customer but could just as easily be someone looking for mattress dimensions or where to recycle a mattress. Think about the buy words associated with your product or service and optimize your site based on those keywords.

Where and how often to use keywords

Back in the 1990s, you may remember seeing a paragraph full of keywords on the bottom of many websites. Twenty years ago, it was all about getting your keywords on your site as often as possible, even if that meant repeating them over and over. The search engines have smartened up since then. Not only does that strategy, called keyword stuffing, no longer work, but it can also get your site pushed to the bottom of the results — a place you do not want to end up.

Today's websites need to have the appropriate keyword density, a term used to describe the ratio of keywords to other content on your site, both in the body of the site that is visible to your visitors and in the code that is geared toward the search engine robots. While every word on your site is a search term for a user to find your site, your site will no doubt mention key phrases quite often. These terms, whether they are descriptions of your product's features or of your company's process, are the terms you need to be cautious of overusing. However, the search engines themselves are very tightlipped about their algorithms, as they compete with each other on the relevancy of their results. So, determining keyword density is not an exact science. Instead, it is a fluid process that relies on trial and error. Generally accepted best practices in the search engine optimization (SEO) community say a site's keyword density should fall anywhere between 1 and 3 percent, though some search engines favor even higher percentages.

There are several free tools available online to calculate your site's keyword density. Keyword Density (**www.KeywordDensity.com**) analyzes your site side by side with a competitor based on the specific keywords you want to track. The keyword density tool from SEO Chat (**www.SEOchat.com**)

takes a different approach by manually figuring out your website's best key-words based on your existing content. Both tools look at keywords across several areas of your site, giving weight to the keywords based on their position on the page.

It is important to remember that not all keywords are equal on your web-site. How you use a word can have an impact on your rankings. For exam-ple, one of the most important areas to include keywords is in the site's **title text**, and there are two types of titles to optimize on a website. The first is the page title. Placed within the HTML title tags on every site is a title for the whole page. This is what is displayed on the top of the browser and should include keywords relevant to the page as a whole. This tells the search engine's spider that you have an entire section dedicated to that topic. Since they want to serve the most relevant pages for a given search, they will rank your site higher based on the title.

The second type of title is a section header within the site's content. A section header carries more weight with search engines than a subhead-ing, which is still more important than the body text. Most often handled through cascading style sheets (CSS), which is the special code that dictates the way different elements of a site should be displayed visually, section titles are given the designation "H1" in the HTML code, which is read by the search engines as "heading one." Incorporating your most important keywords in your title text (headings and subheadings) is a great way to improve your rankings for that specific search term.

One of the other important places to include keywords is within **link text**, which is any plain text on your site that links to another page either on your site or externally. While you could simply put the address of the page you are linking to, editing the text to include keywords is a great way to boost your page's rank. So, to take a fictional Texas-based mortgage com-pany as an example, do not just post a link like www.ACMEmortgagecom-pany.com. Instead, take the opportunity to include keywords that link to the desired page like "Texas mortgage broker." Just as a title tells the search engines that you have a section dedicated to a particular keyword phrase, link text tells them you have an entire page devoted to that topic. It is a good idea to use link text whenever you link to pages within your own site so the search engines know what the page is about.

Last but not least in the keyword pecking order is your **body text**. This refers to the main content areas of your website that are not titles or links. This is normally contained within a paragraph tag in your site's HTML code and might include blog posts, contact information, or other general text. While not as important as title or link text, the body is still a great place to incorporate keywords.

Implementing Other Organic, Free Search Methods

The keywords on the front end of your website represent only one part of the puzzle when it comes to determining your rankings with the search engines. Another key factor is what is happening behind the scenes in your website's code. Keep in mind that search engine spiders do not look at your site through a browser like you do. Instead, they read the site's code, which not only tells them what the front end looks like, but also provides them with other details about your site in the back end of your site. That is why it is important to organize your code in a way that is friendly to the spiders.

Metadata and how to modify it

The value of a website's metadata, the specific code a website developer uses to describe the site, is one of constant debate among search engine experts. This code populates things like the title that appears in a browser, as well as the text shown under your link on a search engine's results page. Google, which is notoriously tight-lipped about its proprietary indexing procedure, admitted it does not consider keyword meta tags in determining its rankings in a post on its blog (**www.googlewebmastercentral.blogspot.com**), though it has not made it clear why it made that change. Some other search engines still factor keywords into their algorithms, meaning you should not ignore them altogether. Google does, however, use the meta description, code which acts as a summary of the website, to some degree, at the very least in its results pages, as shown in Figures 20 and 21. Since the value of this data is a mystery that may or may not have an impact on your rankings, it is worth at least making sure your metadata is well written. Metadata can be edited either in your site's code directly or through many commercial CMS systems.

```
<meta name="description" content="352 Media Group is a professional Atlanta web design company, Florida web
development company and New York interactive agency.  352 Media Group is also a custom Seattle web design company,
Detroit web developer and a Jacksonville web design company.  As a custom web development company and web design firm,
we offer web design, web application development, cd production, intranet design and more from our web design
companies." />
<meta name="keywords" content="web design company, atlanta web design, web development company, florida web
design, seattle web design, new york web development, jacksonville web design, detroit web design, web design firm,
custom web design and development, ann arbor web design, gainesville web design, web design companies, cd production, cd
business card, web application development, intranet design, charlotte web design, las vegas web design" />
```

Fig. 20: A look at the metadata for **www.352media.com** shows the meta description and meta keyword areas.

Fig. 21: The meta description is shown on the search engine results page (SERP) to describe a site.

Fresh content

Once your website's code and content is optimized, you should start to see some results in your search engine rankings. Remember, it can take a few weeks or longer, depending on how long your site has been online. Once you start to rank higher under your keywords, your focus needs to shift to maintain those rankings. One of the best ways to sustain your position is by adding fresh content to your website. Again, the goal of the search engines is to provide the most relevant results to their users. If a search engine's spider visits your site to see nothing has changed since the last time it visited, they interpret that to mean your site is not as current as others that have been updated during that same period.

There are several things you can do to make sure your site stays fresh. When you launch a new product or service, create a new page about it. Good text links from other relevant pages will help it get indexed and will help your site as a whole. You should also set aside time each month to make sure your company information is up to date. Add new clients to your portfolio or staff members to your personnel page — even little changes go a long way.

Inbound Link Strategy

Just as linking your site's pages internally with good link text can give your rankings a boost, so can building good links from other sites. If another site links to yours with one of your keywords in the link text, it tells the search engine that your website is a good resource on that particular topic. In a sense, each inbound link acts like a vote for your site. While more links are certainly good things, there should also be a focus on the quality of your website's inbound links. Just like the other SEO tactics, it is not an exact science. There is no perfect ratio for your inbound links. Instead, you should focus on a good balance, and here is why:

Links are hard to come by. Sometimes a link comes naturally — say, from a blogger talking about your company. Others come through a link exchange where you provide a link in return for one to your site. Others still can even cost money, with reputable sites selling off the prime real estate on their pages for search engine marketers to purchase. Because links are so difficult to come by, you should take them however you can get them.

At the same time, relevant links carry more weight than a random link from an unrelated website. For example, if you are an auto dealership, a link to your site from an automotive trade publication is more sought after than a link from your friend's furniture business. If links are votes for your site, links from within your industry is the equivalent of stuffing the ballot box. To go a step further, a link from the most-read automotive publication in the country is even better. Search engines see links from other sites with strong rankings as trustworthy. Therefore, a referral from them goes a long way. Links like these are rare and can come from your company being written about in a magazine or national news site, leveraging relationships with your major suppliers or partners, or by paying for them. And just like with internal links, do your best to get link text in your inbound links. Well-formatted links are one of the most valuable gifts your website can receive.

You should exercise caution when building your links. There are some links that can actually get you into trouble. There are always companies breaking, or at least bending, the rules. The search engines are constantly one step behind, updating their formulas to reward good behavior while penalizing others. During 2008 and 2009, many website owners were reaching out to bloggers with good rankings, paying them for links back to their sites. This practice of link building worked well for many companies but has since not been as effective because the search engines became aware of these tactics and have made changes to accommodate for them, just as the

Federal Trade Commission has cracked down on sponsored posts passed off as unsolicited endorsements.

The Role of Website Features in Search Results

You now know the role fresh content can play in earning good rankings in the search engines. However, there is still one major hurdle in making that happen: your time. This is where some of the dynamic features of your website can make a big impact. The term dynamic refers to those pages that are database-driven — the opposite of which are static pages, which contain mostly plain text and graphics without any interactivity. Many dynamic features allow you to manage your website's content without knowing any coding language (like HTML) through a password-protected administration area. Not only does this make adding fresh content less time-consuming but, depending on the feature, it can also be done automatically.

Dynamic, fresh text

While practically anything can be custom programmed on a website, there are certain common features that stand out when talking about fresh content. Two of the best examples are news/press release areas and event calendars. The problem many companies face is that their products or services are permanent, not lending themselves to frequent updates. Using a press release database allows you to still add fresh, relevant content to your site. Posts can be as simple as announcing a new hire or a recent customer acquisition, all the way up to unveiling a new product launch.

Setting up a press release database is a relatively simple task. Some CMS components have news and press release functionality built in. Another option is to simply create a new page within your CMS to list all your press releases. Then, as new releases are written, you would just add that link to the top of the list. While this option is free, it may also take more time to maintain. Adding a dedicated news database component to your site can set you back anywhere from a few hundred dollars to about $3,000 upfront but can help you reduce the upkeep time down the road. These components will often automatically order the press releases chronologically, even moving older posts to an archive page after a designated time period or number of posts. They can also break the releases into categories, automatically create summaries based on a specified number of characters, and even integrate RSS, which is described later in this chapter, to push out the content to your audience.

Most visitors to your website will never read this content — which may be a harsh reality to accept — but the search engines will. Maintaining good keyword density on these pages will maximize their effectiveness. This is also a great opportunity to take advantage of title text, as illustrated in Figure 22. Not only will this highlight the text on the page for the search engines, but most Web developers will set the article title to display as the page title and within the page's address, making what you write even more important. For example, instead of titling the article "ACME Company Hires a New Account Manager," try instead "Educational Children's Toy Manufacturer ACME Company Adds Account Manager for Phonics Games Team." Yes, it is a long title, but remember the audience: Getting keywords like "educational children's toy" and "phonics games" will draw in better results under those terms.

Fig. 22: A news article showing the title featured not only as the page title but also in the site's Web address.

But there is such thing as a title that is too long. While it will not hurt your rankings, it will not help, either. The World Wide Web Consortium (W3C), which develops international standards for the Web, recommends the ideal title is less than 64 characters in length on its website (**www.w3.org/Provider/Style/title.html**). Again, it is not because longer titles will hurt your site, but many search engines will simply ignore the excess. For example, Google will display only the first 66 characters of a title tag, as illustrated in Figure 23. That is why you should always frontload your titles with the most relevant search terms if you cannot get your title under the character limit.

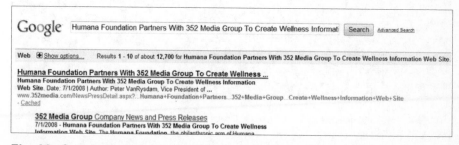

Fig. 23: Google truncates page titles to only show the first 66 characters.

Another way to take full advantage of features like news or events on your site is to link them from your website's homepage. More often than not, your homepage will have the best rankings of all the pages on your site. Knowing that the search engines spider higher-ranked sites more often to check for new content, it stands to reason to put your fresh content where it has the best chance of being seen. When developing a feature like this, ask your developer to integrate the newest articles into your homepage, like in the example shown in Figure 24. This will bring the spiders into these pages more quickly. Remember the importance of links as a virtual vote for a page: A link from your most important page will give the subpages a better chance of earning high rankings.

Fig. 24: The site for sports reporter Amber Wilson dynamically pulls the latest news to the lower left of the homepage.

Programming features also have the ability to let your site's visitors create fresh, new content for you. By integrating things like polls and discussion boards in your site, you are not only reinforcing your position as a hub of information about your industry, but you are also leveraging your users' feedback for your own search engine results. Try to keep as much of this information public as you can to take full advantage of this content. Search engines, just like other visitors to your site, cannot see information you keep in a password-protected area of your site.

Fig. 25: This RSS symbol lets users know they can subscribe to specific content that can show up on their website.

A third way to use your site's functionality to generate fresh, relevant content for your website, which is often overlooked but very easy to implement, is to simply pull in content from external sources. There are several tools you can leverage to draw information from outside your own site into your page. A great example of one of these tools is an **RSS** reader, which pulls information from your blog or other sites onto your site. RSS (really simple syndication) is an industry-standard platform used to publish content that is constantly being updated, like blogs, news headlines, and even audio and video. Many sites make their RSS feeds available for others to add to their own site. Just look for the RSS icon, shown in Figure 25. When a change is made from the publisher, it is automatically pushed out to the various RSS readers, resulting in updates to your site's content. Even though these updates involve no time for you, they still carry significant weight with the search engines that simply see new information on your site.

When to Expect Results

In a world where we have become conditioned to expect immediate results, there is at least one notable exception: the search engines. You can do all of the things recommended in this chapter today, and you would not see any change tomorrow. Indexing is not immediate, and even after the updates are indexed, the search engines must weigh the changes to your site with several other factors in determining your website's ranking for a given keyword. They look at what was changed, how long it was since your last update, how long your site has been online, and what changes your competition makes — and just because they have looked at your site does not mean they have had a chance to process all of the information they found.

This is not a reason to give up. Instead, it is a reason to do more. If you see a small bump in your rankings from one change, you should expect a bigger one from the next change. The results are exponential because the search engines index what they deem active sites much more frequently. You might start moving up one spot at a time, but by keeping up the routine, you could soon be jumping several pages after each indexing. This explains why you will sometimes click on a search engine result and not find the content described on the results page. The site has been updated and not re-indexed. This is why Google makes a cached version available, which is basically a snapshot of the site at the time it was last indexed.

Results can take weeks or even months to appear. And once they do, the cycle will begin again. You will need to identify where your site moved up and where it fell. Once you make your tweaks based on those changes, it is time to wait again. Therefore, the better question is not when will you see results; instead, you should understand when and how often the search engines are looking at you.

The spidering process

The search engines are constantly scanning the Web and creating a record of what they have discovered, a process called crawling or **spidering**. Since their goal is to deliver the most relevant results for a query, it is in their best interest to monitor these changes as quickly as possible. With new sites coming online every day, old ones falling offline, and updates to existing pages, expecting search engines to catch changes in real time is unrealistic. Understanding your site's **crawl cycle**, the time between each visit from a spider, is a great way to understand what, if any, effect your efforts have had on your results. Many analytics tools, like ClickTracks Pro show in Figure 26, have specific reports to show search engine spider activity on your site. *Setting up website analytics software on your site will be covered in depth in Chapter 11.*

If you have noticed one common theme in this chapter, it is that the search engines themselves tend to be tight-lipped about their processes, and how they determine their crawl cycle is no exception. According to a post on Google's Webmaster central (**www.google.com/support/webmasters**), "Crawls are based on many factors such as PageRank, links to a page, and crawling constraints such as the number of parameters in a URL. Any number of factors can affect the crawl frequency of individual sites." In other words: whenever they want to.

While there is no clear-cut number dictating a good crawl cycle, there are some benchmarks available by which you can measure your site. Within your website's logs, available either directly from your Web host in raw form or through an analytics program that monitors traffic, each visit to your website is recorded. That includes visits from spiders as well as from people. Online communities like **www.SEOmeter.com** have compiled that data from members that chose to participate to determine their average crawl rate at around once every two days. That number, however, should be taken with a big grain of salt. Not only is their sample size low, at around 1,000 websites, but the types of websites in the SEOmeter.com community also skew toward search engine optimization providers. As you may imagine, these kinds of sites use all the tricks in the book to bring the spiders back as often as possible.

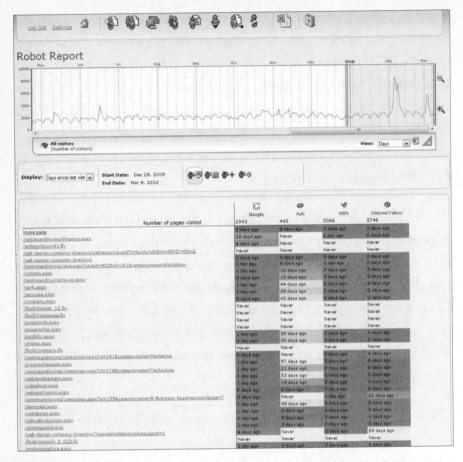

Fig. 26: A snapshot of 352 Media Group's robot report shows some pages are crawled daily, while others are crawled every few weeks.

Based on Google's webmaster tools forum and logs shared by webmasters, what we do know is that the many of the same things that lead to good results — sites with a significant number of inbound links and fresh content — also lead to a higher crawl cycle. However even this is not an exact science. Google for example performs two types of crawls: **deep crawls** and **fresh crawls**.

A deep crawl is an exhaustive indexing of literally every page they can find on a site. The spider will follow every link it comes across to get a complete picture of your site. This happens less often than a fresh crawl, which focuses on those pages they identify as being updated more often. This is how the search engine stays up-to-date on constantly changing sites. Consider the time it would take to do a complete deep crawl of the Web and index the results, and it makes sense why this cannot be the only type of index. The changes that took place during that period would be monumental, and as a result the engine would be irrelevant. This would be tantamount to a retail store taking a full inventory every night. That is why Google and other engines identify the sites that change often like newspapers and blogs, and perform quick, high-level scans on them more frequently. This may explain why content you put on your homepage shows up on Google the next day, while an entire page of content buried deep in your site's navigation may go unnoticed for some time.

Analytics to monitor goals

With so many complex factors at play, it is imperative that you monitor your website's performance, and this section will cover how to stay on top of metrics specific to your website. This may include how people are finding your website, the number of visits, what and how many pages a user looks at and for how long, and where a user exits your site. *Chapter 11 will dig deeper in to measuring your overall return on investment online.*

Many of you may already have an analytics program in place on your site, but you might not be using it to its full potential. With your website at the center of your online marketing efforts, monitoring your analytics means more than logging in once or twice a month to see how many visitors you have had. You could have a million visitors a week and think you are doing a great job. However, your **bounce rate**, or the percentage of visitors who left your site after visiting only one page, could be close to 100 percent. Your conversions of visitors to leads to sales may be tiny. The point is there is more to look at than just the quantity of visitors to your site; you *must* consider the quality, too.

There are literally hundreds of tools available to monitor traffic ranging from freeware to programs costing thousands of dollars a month. However the best combination of cost and features is Google Analytics (**www. google.com/analytics**). Not only is the price right — the tool is 100 percent free — but it has all the essential features of the paid solutions. Unlike many paid options, Google allows developers to build add-ons to its system; if there is a special report you need to run for your site, chances are it has already been made.

A quick glance at the Google Analytics dashboard, shown in Figure 27, gives a great overview of your site's health. In one area, you can see your number of visits and page views, percentage of visits from new users, average time spent on the website including number of pages viewed per session, which pages are the most popular, and how people are finding you. That includes not just what site they came from, but in the case of a search engine, what specific keywords they used to find you. Some of the third-party components described in the chapter may also include their own reporting, but having a comprehensive tool that looks at how each page on your site relates to the next can be a powerful thing.

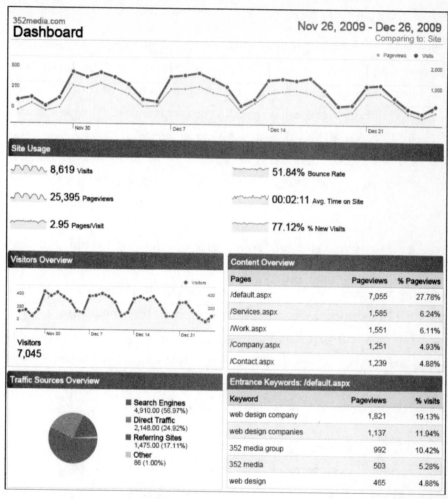

Fig. 27: The Google Analytics dashboard of 352 Media Group provides an overview of the site's performance.

The software also lets you set up reports specific to your site. You can tell the program your goals and monitor the results. For example, if you manage an e-commerce website, your first goal is to make sales. By telling the program the address a customer will see on the order confirmation page, it will tell you what percentage of visitors turn in to sales. The same process applies for new leads, whether that means getting people to complete a form or simply bringing them to your contact information.

How to stay on top

Search engine optimization is a lot like trying to lose weight; not only does it require a significant amount of effort, but once you are done, you are not really done. Once you reach your goal weight, you have to continue to eat right and exercise or you will go back to the way you were. The same is true with SEO. Stop updating your site and the spiders will stop crawling. Stop adding new inbound links and your competition will pass you by. Building a strong search engine presence from scratch is a major paradigm shift that requires you to reevaluate where SEO falls on your priority list.

Laying the foundation for good search engine rankings is certainly the most backbreaking part of the process. Setting up the programming features on your site may seem costly in the beginning, but the return on investment potential is enormous. Once you shift to maintenance mode, much of the work can be automated. Tools like RSS feeds can help you update content easily, and you will find you get more inbound links as your online reputation builds — all without even asking for them. That said, though, there are still some things you can do to try to stay on top.

First off, keep it fresh. While this chapter has talked at length about fresh content in the form of news, events, user-generated content, and RSS feeds, those things focus on your existing pages. It is a good idea to continue to grow your site by adding new pages. If you have a paragraph talking about a service you offer that is well indexed, try creating a whole new page about it. Keep the old content there so as not to disrupt what you have already built, but simply add a text link to the new page. This will reinforce the search engines' decision to rank your site higher for that topic and that keyword.

While strong links back to your website will have lasting effects for your site, you should always be on the lookout for new links to your pages. As you will learn in the next few chapters, you can become one of your best sources of inbound links. By using the right tools on LinkedIn, Twitter, Facebook, and blogs, you can build a wealth of powerful links all pointing to your site. Couple that with links from major news and blog websites — and you will have a great chance of holding on to what you have earned. *You can read more about news and blog sites in Chapter 10.*

CASE STUDY: SEO IN ACTION

Craig Abramson,
online marketing manager
Archive Systems
(www.archivesystems.com)

Archive Systems, a document management and accounts payable automation company, recognized the need to enhance their presence in the search engines. The company was all set to sign a contract with a leading search engine optimization firm for more than $100,000. That is when Craig Abramson, the company's online marketing manager, asked for a chance to try himself.

"I put my foot down and asked them to give me three months to hit our keywords before turning to an agency," he said. "We started to have several budget cuts, so they agreed."

He started with the website's navigation, reorganizing the content, and adding dozens of new pages. Adding complete pages dedicated to a particular keyword, rather than just putting all of the keywords about your services on one general services page, shows the search engines you are a good resource for that topic. Next, he created a list of 20 keywords to focus on. By narrowing his focus, he was able to see results in a very short time.

"Within two weeks of going live with the changes, we were appearing within the first five pages on Google, Yahoo!, and MSN," Abramson said. "We achieved first-page keyword rankings on 95 percent of those targeted keywords."

While those numbers are certainly impressive, it was the impact those rankings had that really impressed his superiors. The site saw a 4,300 percent increase in keyword traffic focused on one of its primary targets, accounts payable-related keywords. Leads rose from an average of four a month to almost 30 for the accounts payable services. Leads related to records storage increased to more than ten per month.

Roughly 10 percent of records storage sales and nearly 50 percent of accounts payable automation sales in 2009 came through the website. To put that in perspective, a records storage sale is typically around $5,000 per year, while an accounts payable automation contract can range from $30,000 to more than $200,000 in the initial year.

Now that he had the buy-in from the company's management, he was given the green light to implement other Web 2.0 marketing tools. He created social networking accounts on the major platforms and started a corporate blog. The company now issues between one and three press releases a month, and distributes them through online services that allow live links back to its website.

Abramson has made believers out of his coworkers. "I'm the only one in my company doing this, and we spent less than $80,000 on the marketing budget the past two years, but still gained more leads and traffic than ever before," he said.

Avoiding the Dreaded Google "Sandbox"

You have seen how search engines can be your best allies in the fight to attract new business, but just like in any relationship, taking advantage of your friends can have serious consequences. In the mid-'90s, many sites found they could increase their rankings by hiding keyword text on their site. They would simply repeat a keyword hundreds of times in a text color that was the same as the background. But the search engines caught on and started removing offending sites from their index. While some Webmasters will continue to play this cat-and-mouse game, it is smarter to stay on the cutting edge of accepted best practices. Search engines will always be one step behind those bending the rules; Google has a nebulous way to deal with sites using questionable practices.

There is a black hole within Google called the **sandbox**. If you find yourself on Google's bad side, you may earn a trip to their mysterious and oft-debated penalty box. Imagine your site is on the first page for your best keywords one day, then gone from the index the next. Many companies have experienced this, and the impact can be fatal for your business.

The sandbox itself is a subject SEO experts do not agree on. However, when you are dealing with the fate of your business, it is better to err on the side of caution. Most people know the sandbox as the holding area where new sites go before they make it in to the search results. This virtual purgatory is said to have originated as a way to combat spam. Someone could simply create thousands of new pages or links to one page on a topic in an attempt to monopolize the relevant search terms. This temporary hold, if it exists, is not what you should be worried about. When an existing site that has been indexed for some time suddenly falls back in to the sandbox — that is what you should be worried about.

In an attempt to keep their results relevant and more importantly fair, Google is alleged to penalize sites that dip in to the gray area of search engine optimization practices. While most Webmasters will seek out legitimate inbound links for their site, there are always those willing to push the limits. If one link is good, then 100,000 would be fantastic, or at least that is the thinking. As rules are broken or ethical boundaries passed, Google will take the necessary steps to make things right. That means blacklisting the offenders.

For the sake of argument, let us assume your site has suddenly fallen off the radar. There are steps you can take to ease the blow and get yourself back in Google's good graces. The first is to confirm your suspicions. It is possible that your competition made significant moves and jumped you. Start by searching not for your keywords, but for your domain in general by using the query "site:yoursite.com" in Google, replacing yoursite.com with your own URL. Take a look at the number of pages indexed, which is the total number of results listed, and compare it to your recent numbers.

If you do see a change for the worse, the next step is to go to the source and see if you are on the blacklist. Simply visit Google Safe Browsing at **www. google.com/safebrowsing/diagnostic?site=DOMAIN**, with your site's URL at the end instead of "DOMAIN." This page will let you know:

- If your site has been listed as suspicious by Google
- If visitors to the site have downloaded or installed malicious software, also called malware, without their consent
- If the site has acted as an intermediary for malware distribution
- If the site has hosted malware

Though this page does not list specific SEO practices like excessive link-building, many believe those offenses can have the same result. If the site has in fact been accused of these violations or of hosting malware, you can request a review of your site on the Google Webmaster Tools site. The best course of action is to take down any recent changes that might be deemed offensive. If you created pages with duplicate content, bought inbound links, or paid for sponsored blog posts about your site, have them removed right away. There is no specific recourse when dealing with the Google sandbox except patience. By removing the offending content right away, you can only speed up the process of being re-indexed.

KEY TAKEAWAYS

✓	Organic rankings, though more difficult to achieve, will cost much less than a sustained pay-per-click campaign. Searchers also view organic results more favorably.
✓	Figure out how your customers search for you. They might not use the keywords you would expect.
✓	Inbound links to your site, especially those that include keywords, are one of the most important elements of any search engine strategy.
✓	Fresh content leads to more frequent indexing and higher rankings over time.

CHAPTER 5

The Benefits of a Business Blog

"An author is a fool who, not content with boring those he lives with, insists on boring future generations."

- Charles de Montesquieu, 18th-century French philosopher

Weblogs, or simply blogs, got their start in the mid-'90s as virtual journals of sorts. Instead of putting their thoughts in a personal diary, early bloggers put their ideas, stories, and experiences on the Web for anyone to read. And back then, there were not a lot of people reading. Today, however, blogging has evolved to a powerful business tool. In fact, studies show that about half of Internet users read blogs. And while there is not a great current statistic available about the number of active blogs currently online, a report from blog search engine Technorati (**www.technorati.com**) suggested there were more than 200 million blogs online in early 2009. Translation: Chances are your competitors are blogging, and no doubt your customers are reading, too. Having a blog is a great way to stimulate your online marketing efforts in a way that will cost you very little money but have lasting effects.

Blogs are not without controversy. Blogs took center stage during the 2000 presidential campaign when, for the first time in U.S. history, Americans were not getting their news and editorials exclusively from the mainstream media. As a result, they took significant criticism from the traditional media, which pointed out the lack of accountability that exists in the professional journalism community. However, comparing the two is unfair, as blogs — for the most part — are not shy about their goals. Where the traditional media offers facts and news about a given topic, blogs have always been a place for opinion. And when talking about business blogs, the opinions should obviously favor the company they are related to. A better comparison for blogs would be to the editorial page, not the front page, of the newspaper.

This fact does not trivialize the role of blogs. To the contrary, blogs give companies access to the opinions of their end users. Anyone can start a blog, and many individuals use blogs as a forum to tout or criticize products brands. Reading blogs from your customers, industry organizations, and even competitors is equally important for companies that want to keep a pulse on their clients and industry.

Determining the Goal of Your Business Blog

There are several benefits your business can see from blogging. The first is very similar to discussion forums. Blogs give you a place to interact with your customers and prospects. But unlike discussion forums, blogs give you more control over the conversation. Not only do you set the topic by writing the initial post, but you also have the ability to delete derogatory comments.

Another benefit of a business blog is the impact it can have on your search engine rankings, which was alluded to in Chapter 4. Blogs, when built as an extension of your main website, play a big role in bringing fresh, relevant content to your site. Blogs give many companies with a static product line a way to get new information on the site for the search engines to index. Just as with the other pages on your site, strong titles and keyword-rich content in your blogs can give your site a big boost.

Determining the goal for your blog will help you determine how to set it up. Some companies start blogs solely for the community aspect, where others focus completely on building search results, not focusing their posts toward actual readers. While both options can be successful on their own, they are not mutually exclusive. When done right, a blog can please both the human and robot audiences that visit it. Regardless of your goal, you stand to have the most success by setting goals upfront for what you hope to achieve with your blog.

Build a community

Blogging is a powerful tool for companies that want to not only position themselves as experts in the industry, but also build a community at the same time. Successful blogs, like other online social and interactive platforms, are designed to encourage two-way communication through the use of comments, links, and reposts. When users come to your site for the first time and see an active conversation with several comments, it can be an indication that your blog offers good, trustworthy content.

Equally as important is posting comments on other blogs in your industry; Technorati reported that 77 percent of bloggers comment on other blogs as a way to drive traffic to their own blog. However, you should not just put a link back to your blog when you comment; instead, offer your opinion on the topic at hand. If you have a post on your blog about that topic, you should link to it, but do not make that the focus of your comment. Simply posting links in a blog comment is known as comment spam and will have the inverse effect you are looking for.

Once your blog has a good following, it can become a very powerful part of your marketing plan. If you have active readers, you can post questions about new ideas or product offerings and expect immediate feedback. And when it comes time for your readers to buy, they will remember the free advice and information you provided. Building a community for the benefit of your customers builds trust and, in turn, should build leads and sales.

Search engine optimization

Blogs are a great way to bring new people to your site, or at least to let them know about your company. The search engine marketing chapter focused on bringing people to your site who are ready to buy, but you should not ignore prospects who are still in the early stages of the buying process. Someone looking to buy a product like an energy-saving light bulb may search by either the product name or description. Hopefully, if your site is well optimized, they will find your product pages, but someone just starting his or her search may use more general queries like "how do I reduce my energy costs," or "eco lighting alternatives." It would stand to reason that if you sold energy-saving bulbs, you should post this kind of information on your blog.

The result is a win-win situation. The customer finds valuable yet free information they were looking for about how to save money. At the same time, you get your product and company in front of someone who may eventually become a customer. Your blog will become a force in the search engines by using the same tactics that apply to other pages on your site, including strong titles, good in-links, and keyword-rich content.

There are also those who will use their blog just as a search optimization tool, completely ignoring the human readers. You can earn good rankings by creating a site with very few graphical elements that is flooded with relevant keywords that links back to your site in several places, but there is no real substance. However, you should consider what happens when someone gets there. Most users, or at least the savvy ones, will recognize the content as self-serving and not informative and immediately click back on their browser. At the same time, the blog will not get as many inbound links from other sites, since it is not really providing relevant content. At the end of the day you may see a boost in rankings, but that boost will be short lived and tiny in comparison to what a well-executed blog that draws readers in can do for your company.

Balancing the two

Finding a happy medium between a customer and search engine blog will yield the best results for your company. If done well, your blog will increase awareness about your company and products, improve your status in your industry, give you direct access to your customers and prospects, increase your inbound links, and increase your search rankings for your relevant keywords. So it is worth taking the extra time to make sure you satisfy both your customers and the spiders when creating a new blog.

Setting up a Blog

Now you know you want to blog, but getting started can be overwhelming. However rest assured that starting a blog can be as simple as signing up for an account with one of the countless free tools available online. As you might expect, you will get back what you put into this process. Using a free tool is a great way to get started in the blogosphere, a term used to describe the collective blogging community, but going with a more robust or customer blog solution can do even more to help you achieve your goals, even if it costs a little more time and money.

One of the big reasons blogging has experienced success is due to how easy it is to get started. You can literally set up a new blog in minutes; it will probably take you longer to write your first post than it will to set up your blog. Maintaining it is another story, one that explains the blog fade phenomenon where blogs are started and soon abandoned. These tools are referred to as "software as a service," or SaaS, models. Some of the big players in the industry include Blogger, WordPress, TypePad, and Microsoft's Live platform. Each of these tools allows you to create a free account and begin blogging right away. They also include the most important features like comments, archives, search tools, and the ability to incorporate videos and photos on your posts. There are also several plug-ins and design templates created by third-party developers to add even more features to your blog.

While offering a great platform for first-time bloggers, these tools do have their drawbacks. Some limit the amount of free storage space they provide, while others limit what you can customize within the design. Another thing to look out for is advertising. Some blog engines will insert contextual ads on your site. This may seem harmless, but consider that these ads are determined by the keywords within the content of your posts. Now imagine seeing your competitors' ad on your own blog.

SEO benefits of your blog on your domain

The main drawback of the free tools, at least the way most people use them, is with the domain name. If you start a blog using the WordPress service, your blog's address will be http://blogname.wordpress.com. That page will get indexed in the search engines, likely very quickly, because of the popularity of the WordPress engine. However, in addition to building a community, one of the goals of your blog is to help your search engine rankings. While you will be able to include links back to your website, you are not actually building as much search engine clout as you could be.

That domain is equivalent to http://yourcompany.wordpress.com, and it is actually a part of the main WordPress domain, not your company's. While you are adding great content, all you are really doing from a search engine perspective is building up WordPress's status. In order to fully realize the SEO benefits of your blog, you need to bring the blog engine under your domain; for example, http://yourcompany.com/blog or http://blog. yourcompany.com. Some of the tools that provide the SaaS options do allow you to host the tool at your own domain, though these may no longer be free. TypePad, for example, charges $90 a month for business blogs that point to your domain name. This gives you the power of a well-known system while allowing you to reap all the benefits of an internal blog.

Another detail to consider is your blog's design. While the SaaS options give you some design control, you are still limited within the platform. While you do not necessarily want your blog to look exactly like your corporate website — you want it to be clear to your users that they are in a different area — you do want to carry the same concept across to your blog. By bringing the blog to your domain, you have greater control over the design elements within the blog.

In addition to freeing yourself from any terms or conditions imposed by the SaaS providers, you are also freeing yourself from advertising. You may choose to post ads on your blog, but now you can control what type of ads will run and, even better, you will get the revenue for those ads.

Pushing fresh content to your site

Even with the benefits of bringing your blog in-house, you may decide you want to start with a SaaS model since it is a great way to get your feet wet with blogging. When you do decide to make the jump to your own domain, most blog platforms allow you to take an export file with all your content so you do not have to start from scratch.

Even if your blog is hosted under a different domain, you can still take advantage of the fresh content on your main company site. One feature that makes blogs unique from other websites is that they will produce an RSS feed of the content that allows readers to take in the content either on your blog, in their e-mail, or through a variety of other programs that are notified every time you post an update to your blog. You can also take advantage of this feed to bring your content to your site, as shown in Figure 28.

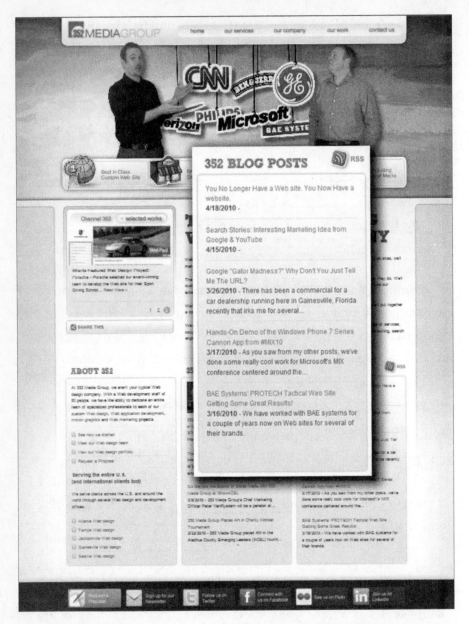

Fig. 28: Bringing your latest blog posts to your homepage not only gives the page fresh content, but it also directs spiders to your blog. This image shows an enlarged look at the recent posts on 352 Media Group's website.

By setting up an RSS reader on your homepage, your site will automatically be updated with the latest content as you create new blog posts. Keep in mind that the search engines frown on duplicate content, so your best bet is to simply post the title and a few sentences from the post to your homepage with a link out to the actual blog. This will keep new information on your most indexed page and will also direct the spiders from your site to your blog to ensure it is well indexed.

What to Write for Your Blog

Setting up your blog is easy, but figuring out what to write about is the concern that keeps many small businesses from starting blogs. Creating a blog that you never update would be worse than not creating a blog at all. However, coming up with topics is simpler than most people think. You do not need to be a great writer to write a blog; remember that blogs are more editorial than news. Regardless of what you decide to write about, make sure it stays within the boundaries of what you have decided your blog will be about. The narrower your focus, the better your site will rank within that category.

Another concern about writing for blogs is how you will find the time. One solution is to take things you would already be doing and turn them into blog posts. For example, prominent blogger Chris Brogan (**www.chrisbrogan.com**), whose blog ranks in the top ten of Adage's Power 150 daily rankings (**www.adage.com/power150**), suggests identifying questions you find yourself answering quite often by e-mail or on the phone and simply posting the response to your blog. "People who arrive via Google by searching for similar information can visit and post comments weeks, even months, later," Brogan and Julien Smith wrote in their book *Trust Agents: Using the Web to Build Influence, Improve Reputation, and Earn Trust.* "…You only respond once — and you get credit each time someone new discovers the answer."

This same model can be applied to other common occurrences at your company. Consider what concerns your potential customers commonly bring up, be it location, cost, value, or problems. By putting these topics on your blog you not only create a lasting resource you can point your leads to, but you also create a tool new prospects can use to find you. Once you start to look at your everyday tasks from that perspective, the ideas will begin to flow.

Reaction posts are another simple way to bring fresh and interesting content to your blog. If you read an article in a trade publication, on another blog, or even from the national media that you think is of interest to your audience, write about it. Let your readers know if you agree or disagree with the conclusions and why. By quoting and linking back to the original post, you can create an informative post in just a few minutes. Posts can also simply be questions. For example, you might ask your readers their feelings about a recent industry trend. Not only does this engage your audience, thus encouraging them to comment and even pass along the post, but comments count as fresh content too. Even though you control the direction of the conversation, an effective blog needs to be a two-way discussion.

With that in mind, the same rules apply to blogs as they do to forums. While your software may give you access to delete posts that criticize your viewpoints or even your products, just because you can does not mean you should. Resist the temptation to remove them. Instead, use them as an opportunity to start a dialogue with that person. Again, you may be surprised by the response from your other customers. Dealing with negative comments can give you an opportunity to address concerns others may have but chose not to write. At the same time, deleting a negative comment will only further incense the author. While you can moderate their post on your blog, you cannot control what they say on their blog or on Facebook, Twitter, MySpace, LinkedIn, or any number of other sites where they may be active. By addressing the comment where it was made, you stand the best chance of limiting the problem from spreading to places you cannot control.

A few things to stay away from with your posts are press releases or blatant product pitches. These things have a place on your site, but not within the blog. People come to and follow your blog to hear your opinion as an expert in the industry, not to be bombarded with pushes at what they need to buy next. The blog is a way to build that relationship so that when your reader is ready to buy, they do not think twice about who to buy from. Taking advantage of that relationship with a sales pitch will diminish the trust you spent your time building.

While the hard sell is frowned upon, that does not mean you cannot put information about your products or services on your blog. But rather than simply touting your product as the best around, consider posting a video demo or product review. You should also link to articles or other blog posts that review your company. This way you are getting the message to your customer without saying it yourself. Customers have a tendency to trust the unbiased reviews.

Keyword-rich titles

The title of your post — just as is the case with other titles on your website, like your press releases — is an area that has significant impact on the post's search engine rankings. Title text carries more weight than the text of the post itself, so use that opportunity to include key terms that people may search for related to the post. For example, do not write a title that says "My Thoughts on This Week's Industry News." Instead, you should cite specific terms you are talking about, like "Thoughts about New Legislature Governing Credit Card Companies." If you are interested in this news, chances are others are too. And if they are interested, they may be searching for information about it. Just look at the example in Figure 29 that uses an industry term from publishing and Web development in the title in an attempt to bring in more readers. By working those keyword phrases in to your title, you stand a better chance of coming up when those people search.

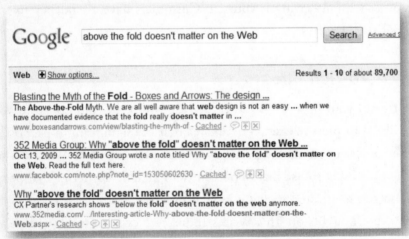

Fig. 29: Good blog titles have a great chance of making their way to the top of the search engines, as in this 352 Media Group blog post, which shows up twice in the first three results.

Have a personality

You already understand that blog posts are more editorial in nature than a news article or a press release, so remember that when you are writing. Most people would rather read a novel than a textbook, and customers are no exception. They prefer to interact with people rather than companies, a topic we will investigate much further in the chapters on social media. They have been conditioned to expect this from blogs. Remember: They started as personal journals written by individuals.

With that in mind, let people know who you are, what your role is at your company, and what you plan to blog about. Blog posts should always be written in the first person. Do not be afraid to insert your personal anecdotes and opinions as they relate to the topic at hand. Adding personality to your posts is what people will remember. That is what will keep them coming back. While a blog might be considered an extension of corporate communication, the same rules do not apply. So, have fun with your posts.

A great example of this in action comes from a brand called Safariland (**www.safariland.com/blog**), a company that makes everything from body armor to holsters for law enforcement agencies. While it is a subsidiary of the multi-national defense company BAE Systems, its specific product group operates like a small business. One of the most frequented posts on the blog is about the problems with carrying a concealed weapon, which focused specifically on the problems a person might have in a bathroom stall. This fun post not only got users engaged in the comments with their own experiences, but it also showcased a special holster the company makes that would keep your handgun from hitting the floor as you drop your trousers.

Links, images, and videos

Blogs are typically very long pages, listing the most recent ten or more posts on the first page. If every post is simply text, this can intimidate a new visitor. The quickest solution is to incorporate links in the text. This also gives your readers the ability to dig deeper in to the information you are providing. While you are at it, make sure to include links back to other related posts or even other pages on your site that offer more detail.

Adding pictures is another great way to break up the text to a more digestible format. Include your own pictures or use an image search to find relevant graphics. However, make sure you give credit to the source of the photo with a link if you end up simply using an image from a search on Google or Bing. You can also use photos with a creative commons license. These images, which you can search from **http://search. creativecommons.org**, are created by other individuals who allow public use of their work. Be sure to check the specific image though, as some are limited to non-commercial use only. As a last resort, you can use a site like iStockphoto (**www.istockphotos.com**), which has small royalty photos available for less than $1 in some cases. Adding color to the site will make it less overwhelming to a new reader and may help them quickly locate the topic they are looking for.

Videos are an even better way to break up the monotony of text while also offering more detail about a topic. The best part of videos is that they can be included inside your site. While clicking on the video player take users to a separate page, possibly one on a different site, videos give your readers more information while keeping them on your website. Most major video-sharing sites give you the HTML code to embed the player on your site, which is as simple as cutting and pasting it in to your blog editing software. This will literally embed the video on your site, though all the heavy lifting of the video streaming is still handled by the source. One thing to keep in mind is that some video players include ads or links to other videos, so make sure the videos you are posting do not link to ads or videos from your competition by watching the full video before posting it on your site. Think of video as you would pictures or articles: Choose things that you think are interesting to your audience or that add humor and personality to the blog post.

Frequency of posts

There is no steadfast rule about how often you should blog, but there are some things to keep in mind. First, think back to your goal. If you are trying to build a community and a strong following with your blog, you want to post often enough so as not to lose the interest from your readers. At the same time, you do not want to overwhelm them with new posts. Remember that not everyone reads your blog posts on your blog. People may subscribe to get the RSS feed by e-mail, and several posts each day would mean several e-mails, which could cause readers to unsubscribe, especially when e-mail overload is so prevalent.

You should also consider the type of posts you write. If you write long articles that are very detailed, you can get away with posting less frequently. However quick reaction pieces or links to other articles do not have as much substance, meaning you should post more often. You can also mix these two styles, writing longer posts when you have the time or a good topic and shorter ones when you are in a pinch but want to keep the site fresh.

There are similar issues with frequency when considering the search engine ramifications with your blog. It is a good idea to make sure the search engine's spiders have something new to see each time they visit the site. Remember that more active pages are indexed more often, leading to better rankings. *Figuring out how often the spiders visit your site requires looking at the server logs or installing a tracking or analytics tool, which will be detailed in Chapter 11.*

Regardless of the goal, a good rule of thumb is to blog at least once a week. This should keep both the search engines and your readers engaged without overpowering them — and that means a stronger community and better rankings.

Getting the Most Out of Your Blog

Now that you know how to start a blog and what to write about, it is time to focus on maximizing the return on your investment. There are countless widgets and tools designed to promote your blog, but not all of them are worth your time. There are, however, some main features that are important to incorporate into your blog. Not only do readers expect them, but they can also boost your traffic and help your blog grow.

Blog roll

Your blog's readers are obviously interested in what you have to say, and they may be interested in learning more about your industry or some of the other companies you work with. A blog roll is a list of other blogs you like. Take a look on the side of most blogs and you will see a list with either a title or the name of the bloggers with a link to their posts. While blog rolls are a great way to share different perspectives with your readers, they also serve as a great way to earn some reciprocal links.

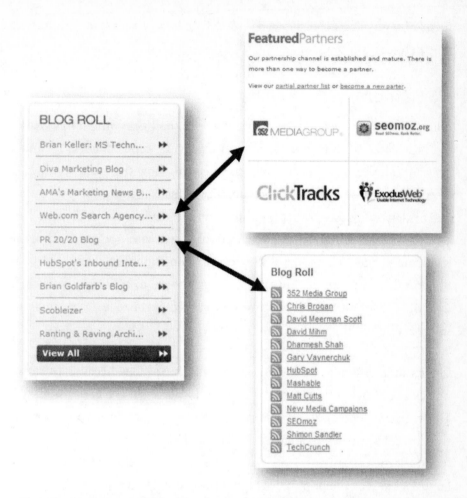

Fig. 30: Bloggers typically link to those sites that link to them, as you can see from these blog rolls from three different companies. 352 Media Group's blog roll on the left links to both PR 20/20 (**www.pr2020.com/blog**) and Web.com Search Agency (**www.submitawebsite.com/blog**), who both link back in return.

As much as you would like to believe that bloggers link to bloggers they like best, most links are only there as part of a blog-sharing agreement. Reach out to your partners, vendors, and other business contacts and offer them a link on your blog roll in exchange for a link from their site, as shown in Figure 30. At the same time, you should not overdo it. Links from sites that relate to or compliment your industry will reinforce the focus of your blog's topic, but conversely, links from irrelevant industries may detract from that.

RSS feeds

You read about how RSS feeds can bring your site fresh content in Chapter 5, but RSS feeds from your blog can also provide some benefits. The main point of these feeds is to allow readers to control how they read your posts. Users may choose to receive your posts by e-mail or in a variety of different readers, including other websites, mobile devices, or even programs on their desktops. RSS feeds are commonly used with podcasts and many major news sites. Users like RSS because it not only lets them read your blog on their own terms, but they can also choose to aggregate your posts with other content to create a custom news feed of the topics they are most interested in without visiting multiple sites.

On its face, this may sound like a drawback of blogs because you cannot control how your content is delivered. However, feeds are more like a distribution network that lets more people interact with your content, thus bringing in new readers. RSS feed services like Google FeedBurner will track the number of people subscribed to your feed, which gives you a good measure of the popularity of your blog outside the site itself.

Comment to build relationships

Most blog platforms will notify you by e-mail when a new comment has been added to your blog. You may be surprised to find comments appearing on your brand new blog, but things are not always as they seem. Spammers, in an attempt to make up for being blocked from your e-mail inbox, have started posting comments on blogs, a process called **comment spam**. In most cases, comment spam consists of a series of keywords and a link to a website and is actually posted by robots, not people. However, in an attempt to circumvent measures to block these types of posts, some spambots will actually mine keywords from your post, adding phrases about how they enjoy reading your posts.

The quickest way to curb these annoying posts is to add a CAPTCHA system to your comment process. **CAPTCHA**, "Completely Automated Public Turing test to tell Computers and Humans Apart," usually consists of an additional field where the user is asked to respond to a challenge question to confirm they are in fact human. More often than not, the user is asked to type in the distorted text, as shown in Figure 31, but simple processes even include a yes or no question asking if the user is human. Distorted text works particularly well because bots just see the text as a graphic, which they cannot decipher.

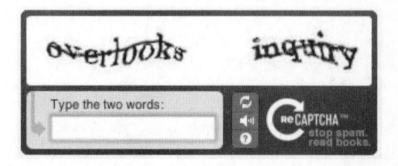

Fig. 31: CAPTCHA programs ask users to repeat the distorted text to verify they are humans.

Another way to limit the effectiveness of comment spam is to add no-follow code to the comment section of your blog. This is simply a line of code that tells the search engines which links to not follow in a particular section of your website. This is also used for sensitive content, including password-protected areas of your website, to ensure the information is not made public. No-follow code will not prevent the comments from showing up on your site, but it will make the links pointless for the spammer.

No-follow code is a good idea because it will also reduce the effectiveness of human comment-spam. Many companies will actively comment on other blogs simply to get a link back to their website. Sometimes they may include relevant comments, but often they will just say they enjoyed the post. It may be difficult to determine what comments are legitimate and which should be deleted, but by adding this code, you at least ensure the spammer does not reap the benefits of their efforts. Adding no-follow code will allow you to control who you want to link to. At the same time, too many outbound links from your site can have a negative effect on your search engine rankings. Simply put, outbound links are a way of telling the search engines that you need to go somewhere else for relevant content.

Promote your posts on other mediums

Now that your blog is set up and you have populated it with the first few posts, it is time to start promoting it. RSS feeds, search engine traffic, and links from your main website will bring in readers, but there are additional steps you can take to build stronger relationships with your readers. Despite what you just read about comment spam, posting legitimate comments on other blogs is a good way to create a dialogue and bring users to your blog. Make sure you offer something interesting in your comment so you do not get deleted. While the other blog may use no-follow code, which means the search engines will not follow the external links from the comments section, you can still get human traffic over to your blog.

You should also promote your blog through other mediums. The easiest way to bring in readers is to add your blog address to your e-mail signature. This lets anyone you talk with know you have a blog. Many people you correspond with may be looking for more information about you or your company, and a blog link gives a way for them to learn more about you personally, not just your company. The same can be said for business cards, brochures, or anywhere else you list your physical and Web address.

Blogging once a week is not incredibly time consuming. At the same time, it is a good idea to encourage others in your organization to blog as well to help share the load. People are particularly interested in what your president or owner has to say, but you can also have your sales staff blog about big wins or other industry trends. Getting more people involved in your blog will make the experience more interesting for the reader while spreading out the responsibility in to a more manageable portion.

KEY TAKEAWAYS

✓	Set goals and a focus for your blog before you start to ensure the best return on your investment.
✓	Free tools are simple to set up, but they may not allow you to take advantage of all the benefits a blog can have for your company.
✓	Have a personality when blogging; readers want to hear from people, not a business.
✓	Promote your blog through RSS, links from your site, and anywhere you list your contact information.

CHAPTER 6

Stop Talking, Start Listening — Social Networks as Focus Groups

"One must listen if one wishes to be listened to."

- François de La Rochefoucauld, 17th-century French author

Marketers are being pressured to "get involved in social media" by the powers that be. As a result, many companies are doing things the wrong way by trying to use tactics that may have been effective on other mediums like television and print. It is critical you understand why people join social networks and what they expect from companies. The key in the beginning is to listen to what people are saying before you respond and offer insight. This is a forum where consumers are providing uncensored and often brutally honest feedback about your business.

An Overview of Social Networks

Social networks, much like Web 2.0 as a whole, are creating buzz among CEOs these days. But chances are even though your boss is harping about the need to get your company in to the social space, he or she is not an active participant there. Most likely do not have a good grasp of just what social networks and social marketing entail — but do not tell them that. Instead, take the lessons from this chapter to become an expert in all things social.

Again, like Web 2.0, there is a rush to jump into social networks. There are more than a few examples of companies that have built profiles on the most popular sites only to neglect them. That is akin to building a shiny new office building before there is a staff to fill it and letting the building sit empty. The first step is to research the market, then get a lot, and finally, only when you are ready, lay the foundation.

The same is true on social networks. Rush jobs and stagnant pages can leave your customers feeling unfulfilled in a medium where they have grown accustomed to instant gratification. Before setting up profiles and sending out friend requests, you need to understand the goal of each platform. Only then can you decide where you company fits best and how you can harness the power of the social Web to have an impact on your business' bottom line.

How did they start?

Social networks, though only gaining wide popularity in the late 2000s, have been around in various forms on the Web for well over a decade. Web communities like GeoCities, now defunct in the United States, laid the foundation for the social Web. GeoCities let users create websites and connect with other users with similar interests. It included chat functionality and discussion boards, much like rival AOL, which peaked at more than 26 million subscribers in 2002.

GeoCities is no longer an active community, but it did leave behind lessons taken by its successors. Much of GeoCities' collapse is attributed to a change in the terms of service after Yahoo! purchased it in 1999. Yahoo! infamously stated all content on the community, including pictures and text, was its property, a decision that was quickly reversed after public outcry. According to a BBC article, Yahoo! officially closed down GeoCities websites in mid-2009. Companies have clearly seen the result of making that mistake. At the same time, these early communities struggled to turn a profit, with ZDNet editor Rupert Goodwins noting in a 2009 BBC interview that GeoCities is "…proof that you could have something really popular and still not make any money on the Internet."

Where are they today?

One of the biggest differences with today's social networks is they are making money. About 20 percent of all display ads viewed in the United States were on social networking sites, according to a September 2009 comScore press release. Social networks allow companies to target specific user groups, since the networks themselves are able to provide a laser-like focus based on the demographic information they collect during registration.

Today's networks also have a better-defined focus as it relates to demographics. You may remember the chat rooms in AOL ranged from topics like "People Connection" and "Friends & Flirts" to "Parenting" and "Diet & Fitness." Instead of just a chat room within a larger community, many social networks today with millions of users started with a specific demographic in mind, and each still serves that group to a degree. You may recall MySpace grew quickly as a site for unsigned musicians while Facebook started as a way to connect with other students at your specific college.

With that in mind, it is important to know who is on each network and what they are looking to do before putting your business there. For example, a T-shirt printing company might appreciate the young MySpace audience while a financial services firm would find little benefit from a page there. It is also important to consider the size of each site's user base, illustrated in Figure 32, when evaluating quantity of users versus the quality of targeting a particular demographic. Although each of these platforms is undergoing constant change, here is a snapshot of the goals, demographics, and reach for the most popular networks.

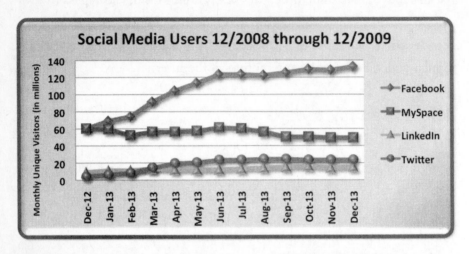

Fig. 32: Based on figures compiled by Compete (**http://siteanalytics.com-pete.com**), 2009 saw Facebook pull away from MySpace in terms of overall visitors, with both LinkedIn and Twitter making significant gains of their own.

1. MySpace (www.myspace.com): While it was intended to be an online storage tool, MySpace quickly evolved into a popular social networking platform in August 2003. Because of the storage capabilities, MySpace was a hit with unsigned musicians who needed a place to not only host their songs but to promote their music. This is still an important part of the site, with many users posting MP3 music files on their pages. After its acquisition by News Corporation in 2005, MySpace started its own record label to help promote artists using the service.

While many of those early users have grown from teenagers to adults since the site first went online, MySpace has struggled to shake the perception that it is only used by teenagers. Digital marketing firm comScore (**www.comscore.com**) found that by the end of 2006, users under 34 accounted for about 46 percent of the site's unique visitors, and people between 12 and 17 made up only 12 percent of the site's overall user base. However, new research indicated that period might have been the peak. Internet research firm Quantcast (**www.quantcast.com**) estimated the site's traffic has steadily fallen since the middle of 2007, in contrast to Facebook's growth over that period; Quantcast puts the audience profile for April 2010 at 76 percent under the age of 34.

Even though there are more adults on the site than most people think, MySpace is not the best place for B2B interactions. The site is set up to encourage interactions based on common interests, but business is generally not one of them. While MySpace's users are passionate, with 18 percent of them visiting the site more than 30 times a month, those users skew toward a middle-income audience, with 73 percent making under $60,000 a year and 64 percent of users lacking a college degree. If your company targets a teen or young adult audience, then a presence on MySpace would not be a bad idea.

2. LinkedIn (www.linkedin.com): Where MySpace had roughly 30 million visitors per day in December 2009, LinkedIn peaked at about 2 million a day that same month. But LinkedIn is not about quantity, but quality. The site, which launched in May 2003, is specifically targeted at professional networkers. The site lets people connect online with their offline acquaintances like coworkers or business partners, known as first-degree connections, in an effort to be introduced to their colleagues, or second-degree connections, and so on until they have built a large network. This is unique to other sites that allow users to search for and request a connection to anyone.

LinkedIn is set up to help professionals build strong B2B relationships or, in many cases, jobs. Companies, school groups, or other organizations can create groups on the site, allowing them to focus on specific subject matter. The site's "Answers" section is also a popular place for businesses to share ideas and practices.

As you might expect, LinkedIn has a much older audience with 77 percent of its users over the age of 35. The site's visitors are also more affluent than MySpace for example, with 69 percent having a household income more than $60,000 a year and 30 percent of users posting graduate degrees. There is a great opportunity for B2B marketers, as evidenced by major advertisers like American Express, Cisco, and Chase participating on the site. For comparison, MySpace has more consumer-focused ads running on their site for things like Best Buy, online camping company Zynga, and auto insurance quotes.

3. Facebook (www.facebook.com): Facebook started as an online year-book for college students. However, the users that were students in 2004 when the site launched have (or at least should have) graduated by 2010. As such, the demographic quickly changed from one similar to MySpace to a more mature and, in most cases, degree-seeking or college-educated audience. Quantcast has the coveted 18–34 demographic at 42 percent of the overall Facebook audience as of April 2010.

Facebook has other things going for it as well, making it a great place for advertisers. Not only does it boast 60 percent of its users earning more than $60,000 in household income, but 66 percent of the overall visitors come to the site more than once a month. Couple that with highly targeted pay-per-click advertising options, and Facebook is a great place for businesses to advertise. There are also other ways for businesses to participate on Facebook by creating pages similar to those individuals can make. These sites, called fan pages, have most of the same features as a regular user's page, with the ability to upload messages, videos, pictures, and — most importantly — make connections. According to Facebook's support website (**www.facebook.com/help/?page=900**), companies with more than 25 fans can even register a vanity URL, formatted as facebook. com/companyname. This makes it much easier to promote your fan page, as the alternative to a vanity URL contains a series of numbers and letters that is not easy for users to remember.

4. Twitter (www.twitter.com): Twitter has a bad rap, but, if used properly, it can be a great marketing tool for any type of business. There is a perception, typically among those who have never logged on to the site, that users are only writing about what they had for breakfast or any variety of other mindless drivel. However thousands of companies — twibs (**www.twibs. com**) has a list of more than 20,000 companies that have registered their profiles as of April 2010 — have seen the power of the micro-blogging engine, which — much like normal blogs — allows users to post and subscribe to short notes fewer than 140 characters long.

It would not be fair to compare Twitter directly with the other platforms because it is still relatively early in its growth, only launching to the public in summer 2006. Another key difference with Twitter is how users access it. While most people read Facebook status updates on Facebook.com, Twitter has been setup to offer a more flexible user experience. An open **API**, **application-programming interface**, allows anyone to create applications to interact with the content posted on Twitter. This means you can use all the features the service has to offer without ever visiting the website. Analyst firm Sysomos (**www.sysomos.com/insidetwitter**) has found that more than half of all updates are published using means other than Twitter's main website. This includes mobile applications, SMS messaging, and many Web-based services. While Twitter is still in the process of figuring out how to monetize the website, which only announced a preliminary advertising model in April 2010, its users have found ways to use the platform to grow their businesses. Some brands have had success posting specials or coupons, most notably the Dell Computers outlet, which has sold millions in hardware and accessories directly attributed to Twitter.

Twitter is also a great place for companies to just listen. Users are talking about your industry and maybe even your products. Some of the talk is positive, and some is likely negative. This is nothing new: People have always talked to their friends about the brands they like or dislike. However, now you have an opportunity to not only monitor those conversations, but also participate. But please, wait until you finish this chapter to start responding to tweets!

5. Aggregators and other tools: There are a variety of other social networking tools available, and likely countless others are still in development. There is a good chance tomorrow's marketing tool of choice has not been launched yet. One current type of site, which functions differently from social networks while still allowing users to share information, is the news aggregator. These sites, such as Digg (**www.digg.com**), Delicious (**www. delicious.com**), and StumbleUpon (**www.stumbleupon.com**) to name a few, allow users to tag stories they find on the Internet. The more a story is tagged, the higher it appears on the website. This allows users to quickly scan these sites for trending topics rather than thumbing through many different sites to find interesting stories. Posts are categorized by topic so users can focus in on the things that interest them. These tools can have a significant — and often sudden — impact on small businesses. Imagine you post something on your website or blog about a new and interesting product. As users come across it, they tag it in on Digg, a process they call "digging." That brings in more traffic and more "diggs." If your article sits on the first page of Digg for a few hours, you can expect a huge spike in traffic to your website. Digg had more than 38 million visitors in December 2009, not to mention users who accessed its content through cell phone apps or other Web-based tools that publish Digg's content.

There is a saying, "hope for the best, but prepare for the worst." That is a great idea to keep in mind while running your business, but when it comes to social aggregators, the quote should read "hope for the best, and prepare for it, too." Make sure you and your servers are ready to handle the traffic spike that these tools can bring. It will not be a gradual uptick in visitors, but a surge that lasts less than a day and is gone as quick as it came.

People Want to Interact with Other People

By now you probably appreciate the important role a social networking presence can play in your company's marketing efforts. But again, resist the urge to jump online and create profiles for your company on all the sites mentioned and any others specific to your industry. Now that you know how significant these tools are, you should learn the ground rules associated with them to ensure your first foray in to the world of social networking is as positive as it can be.

One of the biggest mistakes companies make on social networks, and an easily avoidable one at that, is bringing the same dry, corporate approach to communicating with others. Specifically, they join the conversation as companies, not as people that work at companies. The biggest fundamental to take from this chapter — and maybe even this book — is that people want to interact with other people, not companies. There is a reason you repeatedly mash zero when you call any customer service line: You want to get past the machine and get to a real person.

Take a step back and consider why people join these sites and why they were created in the first place. Mark Zuckerberg, the founder of Facebook, did not set out one night in his dorm room to create a site where companies could connect with their customers. That was likely the furthest thing from his mind. He wanted to create a site where people could connect with other people, in his case Harvard students with other Harvard students. The same is true for MySpace, Twitter, and most of the others. The possible exception is LinkedIn, but even that site is trying to help individuals in one company network with other individuals in other companies.

All of these sites do want to make money, but they do that through targeted advertising or subscription services. Sites that actively try to connect companies to people — there are a few of them out there that you likely will never hear of — are going about it the wrong way. This requires a fundamental shift in the way marketers and small business owners think. You are used to putting your message in newspaper ads or brochures and fliers. Even your website touts the great things about your company (as it should), but that will not work on the social Web.

Think back to the examples of Delta Airlines and Southwest on Twitter. Delta, while improving, still does not follow the basic principle of participating as representatives of a company and not as the nebulous company itself. Bottom line: Planes do not know how to tweet. There are people behind the curtain, and only good can come from making those people known. *Look back at Southwest, specifically their profile section in Figure 5.* The big difference between its profile and Delta's, shown side by side in Figure 33, is that they pull back the curtain, saying exactly who is tweeting on Southwest's behalf. Visiting those three users' personal profiles let you know more about their specific roles at the company. The result is a more personal customer service experience.

Name Southwest Airlines
Location Dallas, Texas
Web http://www.southw...
Bio The LUV Airline! Airplanes can't type so @ChristiDay, @Brandy_King, and @ChrisMainz are piloting the Twitterverse!

8,951   910,616   2,300
following   followers listed

Name Delta Air Lines
Location Global: 66 countries worldwide
Web http://blog.delta...
Bio Onward and upward... News, tips, & updates from Delta. Behind the scenes info @DeltaBlog

246   17,412   812
following   followers listed

Fig. 33: A comparison of Delta and Southwest's Twitter profiles from December 2009 shows a big difference: a personality. Delta has since made significant strides in improving its presence on the platform.

While many other companies are making the same mistake as Delta, there are others doing things the right way. Remember back to Monterey Boats, where Sue Kohler and the rest of the customer service team interact on the owner's area discussion boards under their real names. Or, look at Naked-

Pizza — even though they tweet under the company name, the author's personality is more than evident, with rants about the New Orleans Saints football games and other events local to their store as well as links to photos of the staff members.

Dipping Your Toes in the Water: Listening versus Talking

The rules on the social Web are different than other places online, and to some degree, within each unique platform as well. The rules do not refer to each site's terms of use, but rather the unwritten etiquette that dictates how people interact with one another. You can read articles about how you should network with prospects or customers on social networking sites, but the best approach is to see for yourself as a passive observer.

At its simplest level, a social network is a modern-day focus group, but the feedback you can gather there is much better than what you would get in a traditional focus group. People online are not saying what they think you want to hear. Instead, they are giving their uncensored opinions about your products or services — good, bad, or ugly. That is why it is so important to start listening to the conversations, even if you are not quite ready to participate in them. At the very least, you can take the praise or criticism to make the next customer's experience that much better.

Choosing which networks to join

Most companies do not need to be on every network but should instead determine the best places to invest their time in order to maximize their return. Based on the demographics listed earlier, Twitter and LinkedIn are sites that appeal to most B2B companies, where B2C companies may choose to swap LinkedIn for MySpace, depending on their target age group. Facebook, with its higher-income, higher-educated crowd, is really a good fit for both groups. While joining these sites will give your company exposure to millions of potential customers, you should also be aware of any niche sites that serve your audience or a specific segment of it.

Wikipedia maintains a list of social networks at **http://en.wikipedia.org/ wiki/List_of_social_networking_websites**, including groups for everything from pregnant women, people with disabilities, baby-boomers, Catholic youths, and vampire fans. Virtually every cultural subset has its own site, or at least a group page on larger sites like Facebook. For the purposes of this chapter, we will describe the process to joining the largest networks, as many of the other sites have modeled their processes after these main sites.

Locking in your name

In 1995, it was accepted if your company's Web address was a subdomain: something like geocities.com/companyname. By the end of the millennium, that was considered a major faux pas and was a sign that your site might be less than professional. Now we have come full circle, with major brands promoting subdomains again, as having a Facebook or Twitter page is not only accepted but expected from companies. Take Pottery Barn, for example, which promotes its Facebook address on the back of every catalog as prominently as its regular website. You have likely seen commercials for other major brands where the call to action is a Facebook or Twitter address in lieu of the corporate site. Each of the other three main sites we have discussed also offers the ability to create custom, or vanity, URLs. Locking in those names is almost as important as having your .com reserved.

Twitter and MySpace let you choose your vanity URL as part of the registration process, as shown in Figure 34. Facebook and LinkedIn allow this too, but only for individuals. LinkedIn does not allow companies to set up profiles as individuals, so you need to create a group for your company. *We will look at the steps for that later in this chapter.* Unfortunately, LinkedIn does not yet support custom vanity URLs for groups.

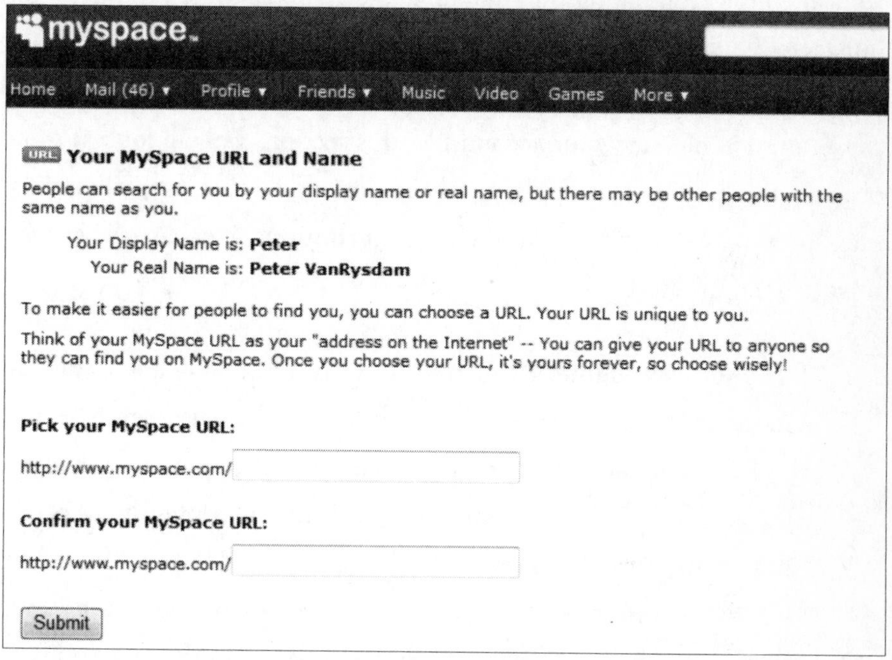

myspace.

Home   Mail (46) ▼   Profile ▼   Friends ▼   Music   Video   Games   More ▼

URL Your MySpace URL and Name

People can search for you by your display name or real name, but there may be other people with the same name as you.

Your Display Name is: **Peter**
Your Real Name is: **Peter VanRysdam**

To make it easier for people to find you, you can choose a URL. Your URL is unique to you.

Think of your MySpace URL as your "address on the Internet" -- You can give your URL to anyone so they can find you on MySpace. Once you choose your URL, it's yours forever, so choose wisely!

Pick your MySpace URL:

http://www.myspace.com/

Confirm your MySpace URL:

http://www.myspace.com/

Submit

Fig. 34: Setting up a custom URL makes promoting your profiles much easier.

Setting up your business' profile on Facebook, while similar to setting up your personal page, has another step designed to safeguard your intellectual property. A new company that creates a fan page must have 25 fans before they can lock in their custom address. This deters people from gobbling up popular names in the hopes of selling them in the future, as is often the case with regular domain names. While this may seem daunting, it can be accomplished relatively easily. From the fan page, you can invite people within your network to become fans, and even include a personal message. Sending this out to your friends and coworkers and encouraging them to pass it along should do the trick. If that is not enough, consider offering a small prize to the 100th person to become a fan of your Facebook page.

Creating your personal profiles

People often rush through their profile setup so they can get started net-working. However, taking the time to create a good profile can have a big impact on your success down the road. While you will be able to edit many portions of your profile as things change, some things like your username are set once you create your account. In this section, we will look at some of the universal tips that apply to all the networks. Then we will address each social network and look at their specific options. Here are the general rules to keep in mind:

1. **Use your own name:** Remember the big lesson — people want to connect with other people. This starts with the username. While Facebook does not let a company create an account as an individual, Twitter does. Grabbing your company name will prevent someone from creating a false profile and posing as you. But you should still have an account in your personal name. That offers the transparency you need on the social Web, and makes it easy for others to find you, as Southwest Airlines does by listing the accounts of the individuals who tweet for the company. With that in mind, try to avoid adding numbers or special characters when possible, like JohnDoe1978. This may be more difficult if you have a very common name, but do your best to create a username that people can easily remember.

2. **Keep it consistent:** When setting up your usernames, try to keep them consistent across every platform. This will make it easier for people to follow you across multiple networks, not to mention it will also be easier for you to remember as you log in to all the different sites. In addition to putting your business online, you are working to create a brand for yourself as the representative of your company. Therefore, you should treat your username as you would your company name and keep it the same across the board.

3. **Use a picture, not a logo:** Sticking with the theme of being an individual, you should use an actual picture and not your company logo for your account. Remember, LinkedIn and Facebook require creating a personal account before setting up your company's page, but even on those pages you should use something different from what is on top of your letterhead. Consider a staff photo or even a picture of you in front of your sign. That way, you get the logo and the personality in. You could also create a version of your logo that incorporates a reference to the platform. If your company has a mascot, that is also something you can use in place of a logo. For example, M&M'S® candies uses its iconic characters from its television ads as social media representatives, which goes as far as having Twitter profiles, @mmsred and @mmsgreen, for two of the more eccentric chocolate cartoons.

4. **Cross-link whenever possible:** Remember that social networks are all about networking. One of the best things you can do to network is to cross-link among your various profiles, as shown in Figure 35. Most people have their personal favorite platform, though they may have accounts on several. Letting them know everywhere they can find you online will encourage them to interact with you on their preferred medium.

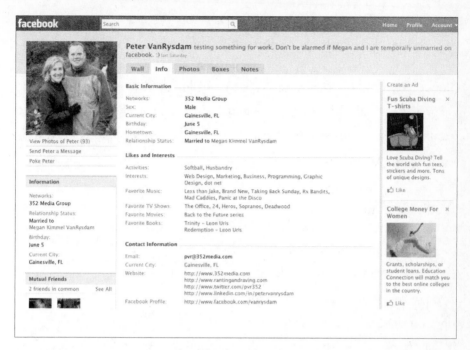

Fig. 35: By adding your other profiles in the Contact Information section on your Facebook profile, users will be able to access you across the other multiple social networking channels.

5. **Write a strong bio:** Some people will find your Twitter account through a search or from another user's post that references you. However, there are many others who will locate you by searching for a keyword that is referenced in your profile. Writing a good bio is a great way to build your network. Most platforms limit your bio's length, most notably Twitter, which allows just 20 characters more than the 140 limit it imposes on your posts. Therefore, it is critical to choose your words wisely. Just as you did on your website, identify the keywords people use when looking for what you have to offer and work those in your bio. At the same time, you should not overdo it. While your bio is important in searches, people will read it when deciding whether to connect with you. Therefore, you should not

just stuff it with keyword after keyword. Instead, intermingle the critical keywords with information about you.

Now that you know the overall rules, let us look at the process for setting up your personal accounts on the major sites. This is all you will need to monitor these channels. *The next chapter will describe the process for creating specific pages for your company.*

As the leader in terms of overall reach, Facebook is a good place to start. Creating an account is as simple as visiting **www.facebook. com**, where you will see a form right on the front page, like the one in Figure 36. From there, you will be taken through a series of steps asking about your education, where you have lived, and much more.

Fig. 36: The registration process for Facebook starts with a simple form to gather your basic information.

This information is used to determine what networks you already belong to. For example, if you graduated from a particular college, you will easily be able to connect with other alumni. Facebook will even suggest friends you may know based on your profile.

Some people are concerned about using their Facebook profile for their business. As you will see in a minute, you need to have your personal account in place before setting up your company's page. If you already have an account, you may have photos or comments from friends that you would not want business contacts to see. Facebook recognized this problem and revamped its privacy options. You can now categorize your friends into groups you create. That means you can show different parts of your profile to your parents, customers, and your college friends.

If you want to create profile filters, the first step is to click on the "privacy settings" option under your account tab in the upper right corner of Facebook, as shown in Figure 37. Then select the first option on the list, the profile information, which lets you determine who sees what. After that you can choose everything from personal information, your birthday, photos, comments, and more. By clicking "Edit Settings" next to any of those options, you can set that information to be shared with everyone, friends of friends, only friends, or specific people or groups you have set up.

Fig. 37: Following these steps will help you control who sees what within your Facebook account.

The process is very similar for LinkedIn, with a simple form on the homepage of its site to start the registration process. Once you have created your account, you can dictate what is shown to people outside of your network. After clicking on the "Edit Profile" button under the profile link on the top left of the page shown in Figure 38, your options are displayed on the far right. From there, you can edit your contact settings or which information shows up publically. Since unlike the other sites, LinkedIn is all about business, there is no reason to set anything as private. Your goal is to gain exposure for your brand, so you should let people know how to contact you and what you do.

Fig. 38: LinkedIn allows you to customize your public profile, as well as who can contact you.

MySpace offers similar controls for privacy. One specific setting to consider is based on age, which allows you to set whether your information is available to children under 18 years old. This is particularly important for businesses like bars or clubs that might benefit from tapping in to MySpace's audience but must also be cautious of violating laws related to advertising alcohol to minors. These settings are accessed from the "My Account" link in the upper right of the page as seen in Figure 39. From there, just click on "Privacy" to view all the specific options.

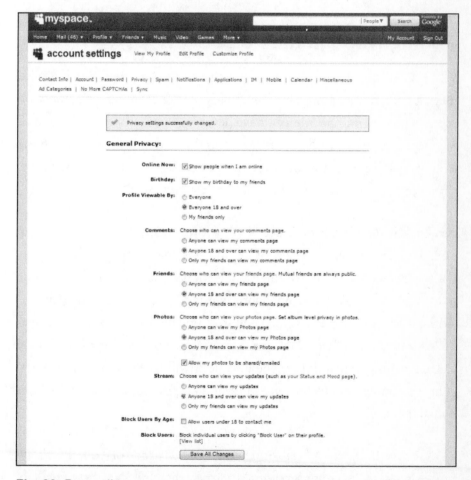

Fig. 39: Depending on your product or target audience, you should consider restricting certain content for minors, especially on MySpace.

Setting up a Twitter account is the most straightforward of all the platforms. Since Twitter is set up as a micro-blogging platform, it is no surprise that the information you can put in your profile is limited. Your only options you can configure are whether to enable geo-tagging, which will track where you were geographically when a post was submitted, and whether to protect your tweets. The protection option is for people who only want to share their updates with people they approve. This is not something you want to do when promoting a business through Twitter. The key here is transparency and access, not secrecy.

Wading Through the Noise

While social networks have many positive things to offer your business, they can come with a fair amount of baggage. You will have to deal with friend requests from people you have never heard of, as well as invitations to join groups, play games, and many other things that will not help achieve your overall goal. Luckily, there are ways to avoid the noise and reduce the clutter by updating your notification settings in the various networks.

Facebook is the biggest offender of all, with so many third-party applications like games, quizzes, and other add-ons that people are constantly notifying you about. Most of these applications' default settings will blast a notification to all of your connections inviting you to add the app yourself. Without fail, it seems everyone has at least one person on his or her friend list who plays every game, takes every quiz, and passes along every chain letter. Learning how to ignore these requests will go a long way to making your time on Facebook effective, while also keeping some junk out of your e-mail inbox.

Click on your "Account" tab in the top right corner of your Facebook profile, scroll to "Account Settings," and then click the "Notifications" tab, as shown in Figure 40. From there, you can select when you would like to receive e-mails. Many notifications, like new friend requests or things related to the groups you join, are worthwhile. However, if your main goal is to use Facebook for business, then you will want to edit the settings for things like event notifications, which can quickly add up in your inbox.

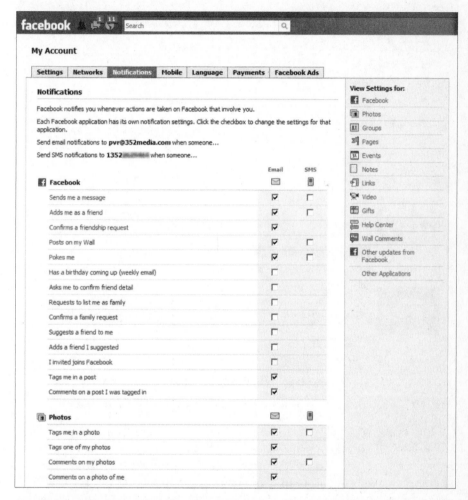

Fig. 40: Facebook will send you e-mails about everything that happens related to your profile unless you update your preferences.

You will likely want to still receive e-mails when a user sends you a message so that you do not miss out on genuine connections, but this does leave you open to invitations to play games or add certain applications. The best way to avoid these is in the notifications page. In small text under the request there is an option to ignore that specific request, block the application, or even block all invites from that user, as illustrated in Figure 41.

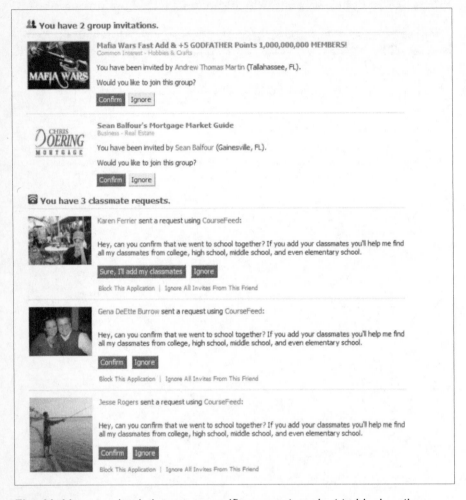

Fig. 41: You can simply ignore a specific request or elect to block entire applications.

While Twitter and LinkedIn do not have the same kinds of applications floating around, there are still certain notifications that can become annoying. Twitter, for example, can let you know by e-mail every time a new person follows you. This is great when you are just starting out, but as your networks starts to build momentum, you could see multiple e-mails every day with new followers. Also, there are applications like Tweet Adder, which will be discussed in Chapter 8, that are designed to help people build their own followers. They work by first following your updates. If you follow them back then they continue to follow you. However, if you choose not to follow them, they will un-follow you. This is all automated, and as such can result in 10, 20, or even 100 or more new followers in a given day.

The same applies to direct messages, which are notes sent privately to you in Twitter as opposed to the public posts. There are applications that will automatically generate a direct message to you in response to you following that person. So assume you have set up a tool to automatically reciprocate anyone that follows you by following them back, which many businesses do. When the auto-following programs follow you, you will follow them back immediately. That triggers their program to automatically generate a direct message to thank you for following them, which may clog up your inbox or cause you to overlook legitimate direct messages.

Everything takes place through programs, flying in the face of the personal intentions of social networking platforms. And at the same time, your e-mail is flooded with impersonal thank you messages from people who do not even realize they are following you. While Twitter may restrict these practices in the future, as it stands now, they are a good reason to stop direct messages from being sent to your e-mail inbox.

As you might expect from a business-focused platform, LinkedIn does not have the superfluous games and applications on their site. As a result, you will not see too many e-mail notifications from them. One common LinkedIn e-mail is a summary of the activities taking place within the groups you are a member of. You can set these e-mails to come as a daily or weekly digest. The settings for this feature are within the specific group and not your general account settings.

Finally, MySpace has what it calls spam settings within your account options. Setting these to high restricts people outside of your friends from sending you applications and other invitations. You can also create a custom setting based on how you intend to use the site. You should also look at the notifications and applications tabs, which restrict their respective categories from overwhelming your inbox.

The surveillance tools

Now that you have all of your accounts ready to go, it is time to start listening to what users are saying about you. But unless you have a bank of computers, a wall of monitors, and a staff to stare at them 24/7, you will not be able to catch everything that is said about your company and your industry. Luckily, there are tools available — the majority of them free — that will monitor the online chatter for you.

Google has a pair of online services, Google Alerts and Google Reader, that act much like your own private version of Digg. They automatically identify mentions of the keywords you specify. It stands to reason that Google would be able to provide this, since they are already constantly indexing everything happening online for their search engine rankings. Google Alerts lets you set a specific keyword through the interface shown in Figure 42, and then receive e-mails either weekly, daily, or as the keywords are found. You can even elect to get the information in an RSS feed. If you are searching for a very specific keyword like your exact company or product names, you should choose the real-time alerts. However, if you select more generic terms related to your industry as a whole, you should go the daily or weekly route to avoid information overload.

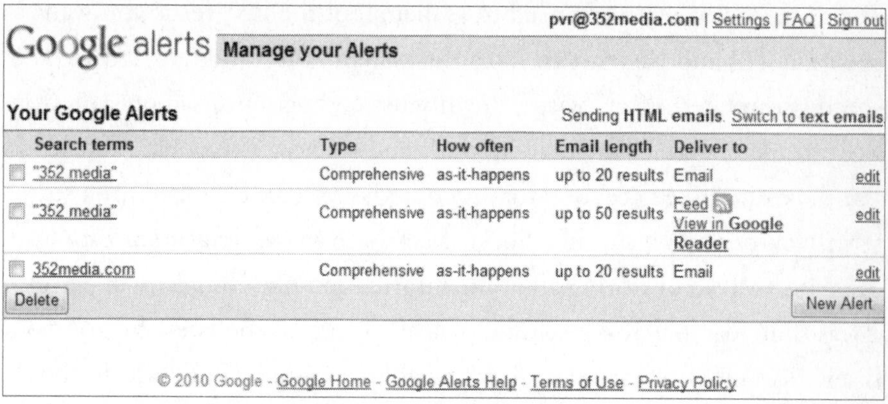

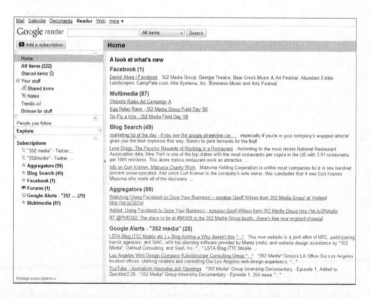

Fig. 42: Google Alerts allows you to set up notifications for as many keywords as you want with settings for frequency and delivery options.

Google Reader works a little differently than Google Alerts, offering a more comprehensive view without the e-mail and RSS option. Instead, you need to log in to your Google account in order to see the information. That makes it not as effective for immediately identifying problems, but it is a great way to get a macro look at the discussion about your company, as you can see in Figure 43.

Fig. 43: Google Reader keeps an eye on multiple feeds that you specify, listed in the left column of the interface.

To get started, you simply need to gather all of the RSS feeds you want to keep track of and paste them in to the system. You can grab RSS feeds of specific search terms on Twitter, any discussion board posts about you from Boardreader (**www.boardreader.com**), and even your Google Alert feeds. For those sites like Facebook that do not give you an RSS feed for a search term, you can use a site like Social Mention (**www.socialmention.com**). This site, instead of storing all of the information like Google, will perform a real-time search across multiple platforms to find the latest hits on your keywords. A look at the list of sites available to monitor in Figure 44 should give you a feel for how helpful this site can be. You can turn the results into an RSS feed that you plug into Google Reader in order to keep all of your information on one dashboard. Social Mention also has an e-mail option; however, it is limited to once a day.

Fig. 44: Social Mention's comprehensive search keeps an eye on all of the major blogs, networks, multimedia, news, and other online tools.

KEY TAKEAWAYS

✓	While Facebook currently stands on top, there are many social networks to consider depending on your industry and your target demographic.
✓	People want to network with other people, not companies.
✓	Learn how the networks work by listening before you start creating your content.
✓	Set up a tool to help you monitor your brand online.

CHAPTER 7

Joining — Not Controlling — The Conversation

"It was impossible to get a conversation going, everybody was talking too much."

- Yogi Berra, Major League Baseball Hall of Famer

Only after you have listened to the types of conversations taking place online can you effectively participate in them. People speak differently online, and not just through the use of abbreviations and emoticons. They speak openly about their feelings on brands, due in no small part to the perception of anonymity the Internet affords us. By not participating in these forums, your company is missing a chance to truly connect with its customers in a way that just is not possible through traditional marketing. Armed with the knowledge of how social networks operate, it is time to join — not try to control — the conversation about your brand.

Deciding on Your Approach

You should have a good idea of how you want to proceed after looking at how your competitors and others with similar business models use social networks. Too many companies bring the push marketing philosophy to social networks, promoting offers that tend to fall on deaf ears. What you need to do is interact with your friends and followers in a way that fits the venue. That means responding to complaints, making the most of accolades, and creating your own content. Remember: This is a dialogue, not a monologue.

What is your incentive?

One aspect of your social networking strategy is predefined: You need to listen and respond to customer service issues. While we will address that later in this chapter, it is now time to decide what else you want to offer to your connections online. You need to provide value in order for people to listen to you. Value can come in different forms, including monetary to informational, and the approach your business takes depends on your overall goals. But regardless of what you decide, you need to execute properly.

One common approach, particularly in B2C scenarios, is to use social media platforms as a way to promote various incentives like discounts and coupons. These have obvious value to your customers, and assuming they are meaningful, they can help you quickly grow your network. One effective approach is to tailor your offers to the medium. For example, Twitter is all about fast and timely communication. People are reading tweets on mobile devices and commenting immediately. The reason companies like Dell continue to have such great success is not just because the offers they give are good; they are also tailored to the Twitter community. One of Dell's multiple Twitter accounts is set up to exclusively post deals from its outlet at **www.Twitter.com/delloutlet**. That means that unlike the normal Dell product you would buy, there are limited quantities on the Dell outlet. In some cases, the offers are on individual items like refurbished laptops or accessories. Those types of specials lend themselves perfectly to a medium based on instant communication.

While coupon codes and promos are good ways to bring people in, you need to remember to incorporate other things in your posts in order to keep people interested. There is little incentive for a Dell customer to come back after they have the product they were originally looking for; that is, unless you can also offer service or support help through your account, which Dell in fact does. Without that, it would simply be a one-way conversation with no more value to the customer than e-mail blasts.

Unfortunately, there are far too many stories of companies that have failed in this regard. While failure for most means simply that no one is listening, in other cases it can be far worse. While customers may share a good offer, an embarrassing or offensive one can spread almost instantly across social networks. A great example of this (or a horrible one, depending on your perspective) comes from Habitat UK, a British furniture retailer, as illustrated in Figure 45. The company used Twitter to push discounts and other offers out to its followers, and it appeared like it was responding to customers' questions. However, it is clear that the company was simply sending the same message over and over to different users. That is a mistake, and one that would likely cost the company a few followers, as more savvy users would immediately recognize those messages as spam. However, that was just the beginning of their blunders. Things quickly went downhill.

Now, take a look at the tweets marked with the arrows on the left. A hash sign (#) and a keyword precedes the same offer. **Hashtags**, (# + keyword), are often used by tweeters to indicate that their posts are about particular topics. If a group of people all uses the same hashtag, it makes it easier for others to search for and follow the conversation. Searching for something with a hashtag helps filter out erroneous results. For example, users discussing a company like Apple may use #Apple, but searches for apple without the tag would also include results about the fruit.

Fig. 45: An April 2010 352 Media Group blog post looks back at Habitat UK's Twitter feed that shows two of the ill-advised attempts to promote its offer.

However in this case, Habitat UK was not tweeting about things like the Apple iPhone (#iPhone, #Apple) or 2009 Iranian presidential candidate Mir-Hossein Mousavi (#mousavi). Instead, the company was looking for the most popular hashtags at that moment and inserting them into its tweets. The hope was that the thousands of people who might be monitoring those topics would see the offer. The tweets were seen, but not by people looking to save 20 percent on furniture.

There was an almost immediate Twitter backlash, which also spread to the company's other platforms. The issues were not only that Habitat UK was hijacking hashtags to promote its tweets, but even more so that the hashtags it was using were about sensitive topics like the Iranian election. Realizing its mistake after seeing the hundreds of irate responses, the company pulled the offending posts from its site. However, it simply replaced them with generic offers and did not address the situation. Ignoring the problem may work in other areas, but not with social networking. This simply meant that all the discussion about its brand was negative.

With no explanation or apology, Twitter users just grew angrier. Comments ranged from people expressing shock and disappointment about the tweets, noting the behavior was not consistent with the quality of the brand. Others were simply angry, accusing the retailer of spamming. Everyone from other marketers to customers weighed in, and not everyone's reaction to the Habitat UK incident was suitable to print, as more than a few tweeters used colorful language to support their opinions. Even worse, the uproar introduced Habitat UK to many people who were not familiar with the brand, starting the relationship off on a terrible note.

Habitat UK did submit a formal apology a couple of days later, but for many it was too little too late. The damage to their reputation had been done. The disappointing thing is that much of that damage could have been avoided with an immediate response to the situation and apologies to those who commented. Before sites like Twitter, companies could take a few hours or even a few days to craft their response. However, thanks to the immediacy Twitter affords, the timelines for companies dealing with crisis communications is significantly shorter. If they had been monitoring Twitter closely, they would have seen the customers were wasting no time posting their opinions.

Since that incident, the Twitter account for Habitat UK is a model of best practices. The contributors are named, their pictures used on the site. Also, the majority of the posts are replies to other users. They now have roughly 1,900 followers, up from the 600 they had at the time of their mistake in June 2009. It begs the question, how many followers would the company have today if not for their poor handling of the incident?

Another content strategy for social networks is to become a resource within your industry. This too can be a powerful strategy to build a loyal following on the networks. Look at the New Orleans restaurant NakedPizza, for example. They have used coupons and promotions to promote their company on Twitter and Facebook, even going so far as taking orders through those channels. However that is only a small part of what they post. The company, which is built on the values of healthy eating and organic ingredients, also posts news and information about living a healthy lifestyle. For example, a recent post on its Twitter page links to an article on Michelle Obama's campaign to fight childhood obesity.

Depending on your product or service, you can also use social networks as a hub for product information. This is different from promoting discounts or specials. Instead, if your product is complicated or unique, you can use these platforms to provide interesting facts. Sticking with the NakedPizza example, it has multiple posts about the unique ingredients it uses, like pre- and probiotics and various grains in its dough. This approach is also good for a very technical product. Rather than waiting for the support questions to come up, address common questions through your social networks.

In either of these approaches, you need to be careful not to come across as insincere. Putting one piece of information among 50 posts about sales and promotions will not do the trick. Yes, this is marketing and advertising, but remember that you need to take an inbound approach here rather than an outbound one. This is your opportunity to build a relationship with potential customers, not to make the hard sell. They will remember you when it is time to buy, and they will appreciate the information they have gleaned from you over that time. Stepping off the pulpit and making valuable con-tributions to the public discourse will pay off in the long term.

The importance of transparency and the backlash of deceit

As a marketer, it is always a big win when you get something for nothing. You can pay tens of thousands of dollars for an advertisement in a national newspaper, but a write-up right next to that ad is completely free. Plus, it has a much better chance of being read and trusted by the reader. This is the rationale behind **sponsored conversations**, a new buzzword in online advertising that refers to paid blog posts masquerading as editorial content. The result can be just as good as the national newspaper article; however, the backlash can far outweigh the potential good.

In a sponsored conversation, a blogger, tweeter, or YouTube user is given a free product sample, a free service, or simply money in exchange for a favorable review. This is something that has taken place for years, with professional journalists given new gadgets to try out before writing a review. While journalists were held accountable for the legitimacy of their reviews, the emergence of unprofessional bloggers has blurred the line. The problem has been, at least until late 2009, that the reader had no way to know what was sponsored and what was sincere. As a result, the Federal Trade Commission has stepped in, modifying its guidelines on endorsements and testimonials. The ruling, released on its website in October 2009 (**www.ftc.gov/opa/2009/10/endortest.shtm**), calls for disclosure of the nature of the post.

What may sound like a blow for advertisers may actual help them avoid a potential public relations nightmare. Without disclosure, you stand to gain great, seemingly unbiased exposure. But consider what happens to the brand if the undisclosed sponsorship is made public. The result would quickly turn from a great endorsement to what may be perceived as an attempt to deceive customers. Just take Walmart, for example.

In 2006, the retail giant's public relations team got wind of a couple that planned to take a recreational vehicle across the country to visit their children, staying in Walmart parking lots along the way. The company offered to provide support if the RVers would chronicle their trip in a blog called "Wal-Marting Across America." In exchange for the posts, the couple received free travel to their starting point in Las Vegas, the RV itself, gas, and payment for each post. All of this is perfectly acceptable, as it is done every day through things like celebrity endorsements. However, the problem was that nowhere on the site did the bloggers disclose their connection with Walmart. They did list Working Families for Walmart as a sponsor, as seen in Figure 46, which turned out to be funded by the Walmart PR firm.

Fig. 46: A screen capture of the now defunct website "Wal-Marting Across America" shows no disclosure either in the posts itself or any-where else prominent on the site.

As these questions came up, the PR stunt quickly went from a campaign that might yield moderate results to a very public black eye for Walmart. Bloggers and journalists who would not have given the blog a second look if it had outlined the relationship between the two parties were suddenly buzzing about the deception. Condemnations came from other bloggers as well as the national media, which likely trickled down to the customers. A simple disclaimer, while possibly taking something away from the blog, would have been enough to avoid a major blunder for Walmart. Instead, the ordeal ended with a simple apology from Walmart's public relations firm behind the blog. Edelman issued a brief statement on its blog (**www.edelman.com/ speak_up/blog/**), taking responsibility for the lack of transparency.

Sponsored posts are not dead; they are just something the public is now aware of. When done properly, these kinds of posts can still be effective. There are several companies that offer a network of paid tweeters on Twitter, who clearly label the posts as sponsored. Likewise, there are sites like SocialSpark (**www.socialspark.com**) that act like ad networks, connecting sponsors with high-profile bloggers willing to take on sponsored posts — albeit for a hefty price, as shown in Figure 47.

Fig. 47: Companies offer sponsored posts in much the same way they do banner advertising, with information about a blog's reach and demographics.

The bloggers, in order to maintain their standing as leaders in their industry, make sure readers will not miss the disclaimer, as you can see on a sponsored post from Chris Brogan's blog (**www.chrisbrogan.com**) in Figure 48.

Fig. 48: Brogan puts his disclaimer above any sponsored post, as well as in the page title and post title itself.

The best approach is to be transparent while also being a resource. If your product is special, it will be buzzed about. If your customer service is top-notch, people will comment about it. But if you try to surreptitiously promote yourself, people will scream about it. Companies should use social networking to build relationships with others while promoting their offering, not as a way to spam a large community.

Much like with blogging, the more people you can get involved in social networks from your company, the better. People expect a certain type of content from marketers, and therefore, they may be more likely to listen to others from your company. While the CEO is the best choice, it is not always a reasonable option. Getting product development, research and development, or the people that actually build your products or perform your services to join is a great way to put a personality on your products. Regardless of someone's role in your company, there is a place for them within the social marketing strategy. In the next chapter, we will get deeper in to how each person can get involved in each type of social network to have the greatest impact on your business.

Populating and Propagating

After being a passive observer on the various social networks, monitoring the conversation about your company and your industry as a whole, it is finally time to start contributing to the conversation. While this can be very time-consuming, there are ways to automate elements of the process without coming across looking like a robot. There are also some great tools to further personalize the experience and maintain a consistent brand image across all of your various mediums.

Customizing your business' profiles

By now, you have set up your accounts following the steps outlined in Chapter 6. The next step is to customize them to incorporate your brand. Twitter, for example, allows you to upload your own unique background image. This gives you an opportunity to bring in design elements consistent with those on your website. Assuming you are linking between the two sites, this will make the transition back and forth less jarring to the user. It will also give them confidence that the page they are seeing is actually yours and not that of a squatter or imposter.

The background gives your Twitter account more than just a nice appearance. It is also a place for you to go beyond the limited bio Twitter allows. While the background is an image and not a clickable section, you should still provide links to other ways to

Fig. 49: Southwest Airlines uses its background to tell its story, promote its other pages, and boast some of its recent recognitions.

connect with your company, as well as any larger pictures or an expanded biography. Just look at the left-hand portion of Southwest Airlines Twitter page, as shown in Figure 49. MySpace also allows for some customization as well, while Facebook and LinkedIn do not give you the ability to modify major elements of the design.

Leverage your existing content

You do not need to create separate posts for each platform. While there are cases where you will want to promote something through only one network, like a contest to get more followers on Twitter or using a feature specific to a network, you can usually cross-populate your content across the various networks. It is rare that a customer will interact with you on more than two of these platforms, so there is not a huge concern about the public seeing the repetition. Leveraging your content to populate every network will keep each loaded with fresh content, which is extremely important when trying to build a following. There are literally hundreds of tools available to share content, from websites and RSS readers to platform-specific applications. Here is a brief overview of some of the most popular and powerful free tools to save you time when updating your profiles:

RSS Feeds

The simplest way to populate your networks is through RSS feeds. In this scenario, your blog is your social hub, pushing out its content to the other networks. Facebook and LinkedIn allow you to insert your RSS feed and then will automatically post your latest blog entries to your status. In Facebook, this can be set up in your personal and company profiles.

TwitterFeed

TwitterFeed is one of many services that will access your Twitter account to import in an RSS feed, something not natively available though Twitter.

When a new blog is posted, TwitterFeed will detect the post and tweet it from your account with a link to the post. You can even set prefixes or suffixes like "My Latest Blog Post" to appear in the tweet.

Ping.fm

Ping.fm is a tool that allows you to post updates through their service that can then disseminate it to more than 50 social platforms, including all of the major services. The tool automatically shortens URLs to fit in the limitations of sites like Twitter, and it can even post photos.

TweetDeck

For some users, you may find you use one network more than the others. If Twitter is your preferred platform, then an application like TweetDeck is a great way to stay on top of it. TweetDeck is a free download built on Adobe's Air platform, which acts similar to Flash but on a desktop environment. It not only manages multiple accounts from one dashboard, like your personal and professional accounts, but also can update Facebook. The best feature is the grouping, which allows you to set up different columns. For example, you can have one to read tweets from everyone you are following, one for direct messages, one for replies, and another to look at a specific group like coworkers or clients. Twitter now offers a list feature like this from their website, but TweetDeck lets you see it all on one screen, as seen in Figure 50. You can even set up columns to monitor specific keywords to keep an eye on your brand.

Fig. 50: TweetDeck is a great way to manage your Twitter account when you follow hundreds or even thousands of different people across different groups.

Creating content relevant to the medium

While tools like Ping.fm and TweetDeck make it easier to push content from one place to multiple networks, there are times when the content should be specific to the medium. The overall goal may be the same across all networks — to publicize your company's products or services — but each medium offers you a unique way to do that. Facebook's fan pages allow you to push updates to your network along with embedded videos, articles, or other media, allowing for a rich and entertaining experience. Twitter, on the other hand, is designed to accommodate quicker, more concise communication, making it a perfect starting point for support or customer service issues. LinkedIn is geared toward professional growth, so more straightforward promotion is not as discouraged here as it may be on other sites.

While populating all of your networks in one move is the easiest way to keep everything current, it is also a good idea to create a plan at the micro level. Take your overall social media strategy, which is in most cases simply to increase sales, and consider how each platform can help you achieve a specific part of that.

For example, set up monitoring to stay on top of complaints or praise on Twitter. Answer questions there if possible, or invite the customer to your FAQs page, discussion board, or blog, depending on where additional information can be found on their specific issue. Facebook is also a great tool to nurture existing client relationships. Once someone becomes your fan, you have a direct line to offer them support, complimentary products, or other information that may lead to repeat business.

LinkedIn, on the other hand, is a great tool to connect with people in need of your services, especially in the B2B marketplace. Their question and answer area is full of people asking about things you can help with, giving you a direct line to people you can connect with and help. From a B2C level, MySpace can also help you identify new prospects. By segmenting your networks to offer specific content while still pushing your high-level message out across all sites, you are able to provide unique experiences for every group you serve.

While your main goal is to increase revenue, there is another overarching goal in social media, regardless of the platform. That is to have your fans, followers, and friends share your messages with their networks. The next chapter will cover how that happens on each network, but the point now is to consider each post, asking yourself the question: "Is this buzzworthy?" Think about what would make you share something, whether it be a unique gadget, a limited-time promotion, or simply an amusing video or article.

Promoting the Positive

Much of the focus so far has been on using social networks as a way to nip customer service issues in the bud. However there are also plenty of compliments to be had there as well. While saying something nice about yourself may come off as conceited, sharing others' comments can act as a strong referral for customers on the fence. User-generated content is what makes social networking and Web 2.0 unique. Finding and sharing this content is not only a great way to help that particular user feel recognized and publicize your achievements but also helps you to offer fresh new content with little leg work.

Simply reposting someone else's praise — or as tweeters would say, retweeting it — is one way to share your success. A better way though is to thank the supporter, including his or her feedback in your reply. This gets the message across to your network, along with a nice shout out to the original author, while not coming across as obviously patting yourself on the back.

Having a conversation with another user is a great way to get your posts seen by his or her followers. However, you should not start your posts with the other user's Twitter name. While some will see it, many have their Twitter feed set to ignore messages that start with someone else's username, as it considers them to be a direct conversation between two users and not something everyone would be interested in. Putting their name, in the form @username, anywhere else in the tweet will get it in front of more users.

While any conversation is a good way to get your name out, imagine the exposure connecting with a celebrity, or at least an Internet celebrity, could bring your business. Getting your message in front of his or her audience gives it a much better chance of getting noticed. By interacting with people who have amassed a huge following, you put yourself in a position to pick up a good number of followers.

Celebrities should not be limited to actors like Ashton Kutcher, the first person to earn 1 million followers on Twitter (he had nearly 4.8 million as of April 2010). There are also celebrities within your industry. Sites like

Twellow (**www.twellow.com**) can help you search for influencers in your world by searching their profiles and sorting by the number of followers. While getting Ashton to reply to you — his Twitter handle is @aplusk — might bring you more traffic, getting someone respected in your field to do the same might bring in more valuable, targeted traffic.

Dealing with the Negative

Republishing the positive comments about your company is the fun part of social networking. Surprisingly though, dealing with the negative ones can also be rewarding and positive if handled correctly. Social networks have given the average person a voice they did not have in previous generations. If a company wronged someone 20 years ago, the worst they could do was write a letter to the editor of their local newspaper or a trade publication and hope it was published. Today, they are their own publisher. Companies should never ignore the unhappy customers, but now it is more than just your conscience at stake, and today's unhappy customer can make plenty of noise.

Everyone has seen something negative written about them, either in his or her personal or professional life. The first instinct is to respond with how you really feel; however, that is rarely the smartest course of action, especially in business. In many cases, you may simply end up drawing attention to a situation that might have otherwise gone unnoticed. And chances are you will come across as the big, bad corporation attacking the little guy, even though you did not start the argument.

What you respond to is your choice. There are certain arguments you simply cannot win. When someone is vulgar or making up information, it is better ignored or left to the lawyers. The better decision is not whether to reply but how to do so. Southwest Airlines has been a great example so far, and they are in this case as well. In January 2010 there was an incident with 80s pop singer Debbie Gibson where she was accused of smoking in the lavatory by a Southwest flight attendant. Gibson tweeted her anger, writing "SW Airlines, accused ME of SMOKING in restroom on plane! I'm SO getter her fired! Naasty!!! (sic) Me?!? Smoking?!?" She went on to write a blog post about the incident.

As you might imagine, Gibson's fans were not as cool and composed as she was. Southwest's social team could have easily found themselves arguing with hundreds of people. Instead they made the right choice by reaching out directly to Gibson both publically and privately. More specifically, they used the mediums Gibson used, allowing her to control the conversation. A Southwest representative commented on the blog post, as seen in Figure 51, and reference it on Twitter.

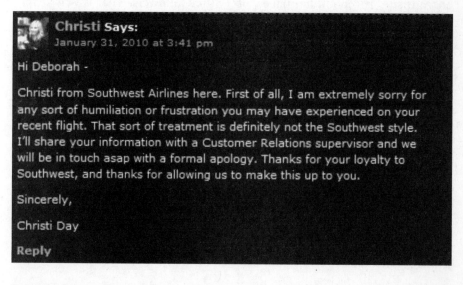

Fig. 51: Southwest's team responded quickly to the situation in a very professional tone.

If left ignored, the responses could have continued to snowball out of control. If Southwest ran to the defense of the flight attendant, they would have created an even bigger issue. Instead, Southwest apologized and promised to look into the situation rather than jumping to conclusions. For all we know she was smoking, but the company took the right approach to assume she was innocent until proven guilty. Gibson seemed to appreciate the response as well, as she tweeted, "Thnx (sic) 2 all from SW 4 reaching out. If she wasn't so arrogant in her false convicictions (sic), I wouldntve (sic) bothered writing!" Terrible spelling aside, Gibson was ultimately pleased with the outcome, and Southwest should be too.

Not responding to a problem does not necessarily mean you are ignoring it. Remembering back to the Monterey Boats Case Study in Chapter 1, the community will often come to your defense. The Debbie Gibson case is not a good example of this because the people reading her posts are mostly fans who are quick to fall in line on her side. But that is not always the case, especially within groups about your products, such as discussion boards on your site, Facebook fan pages, or Twitter followers. That is why it may be a good idea to let the dust settle for a few minutes before posting your defense. A reply from your customers will carry more weight than one from you. But do not wait too long.

Set a schedule

With all of the examples you have seen so far, there is one thing in common: These brands are monitoring the buzz about them, good or bad. While bigger companies like Southwest can dedicate a team to hold watch around the clock, this is not possible in most small businesses. That is why it is crucial to set a schedule to make sure nothing slips through the cracks.

Take time each morning and evening to log in to your Google Reader account to see if anything new has come up. If you have enough alerts through Google Alerts and Social Mention, you should come across anything that needs immediate attention. You can also ask others within your company to help out, whether that be others in the marketing department, your sales staff, a receptionist, or even interns.

The schedule should not just be passive. You should make sure you are updating your profiles at a consistent pace. By using a service like Ping.fm, you can easily keep your site fresh in just a few seconds. Set aside a couple of times a day at the very least to do so. An update can be as simple as a link to an article you read that day or a retweet of someone else's comment about your brand or industry. Keeping your networks fresh, much like keeping your website up to date, will help you hold your audience's attention.

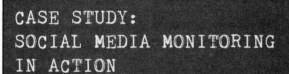

CASE STUDY:
SOCIAL MEDIA MONITORING
IN ACTION

Caryn Kboudi, vice president of
corporate communications
Omni Hotel (www.omnihotels.com)

Negative comments about your company can have a disastrous impact on your business. When handled properly, however, they can be turned in to great public relations wins. That is exactly what happened for Omni Hotels, thanks to their vigilant monitoring of social media buzz about their brand.

When public relations expert Peter Shankman, someone you will read more about in Chapter 10, got ready to speak at the PRville conference at Jacksonville, Florida's Omni Hotel, he ran in to some problems with the hotel's Wi-Fi connection. Shankman tweeted the following to his following of more than 50,000 users:

Who knows if he anticipated the wheels that would be put in to motion behind the scenes at Omni's corporate offices as a result.

In addition to several other keywords, the hotel's staff was using tools like HootSuite and TweetDeck to monitor any hits on the word "Omni." Omni's marketing team had previously made the decision to handle its social media monitoring in-house to make sure it could handle situations within extremely short timeframes, which proved an especially prudent choice in this case.

"Our first step was to determine in which hotel he was experiencing the Wi-Fi issue and to let him know we heard him, so we immediately sent a tweet requesting his whereabouts," said Omni's Vice President of Corporate Communications, Caryn Kboudi. "Simultaneously, we sought to find him via our reservations data. As soon as we discovered he was in Jacksonville, we contacted the hotel."

According to the timestamps on the tweets, this process took under a half hour. By this point, Shankman was already giving his presentation. The hotel used that time to resolve the technical problem and respond to some of his followers who retweeted the original post to let them know they were addressing things. The staff also took the opportunity to box up a piece of key lime pie to go for when he was done speaking.

In response to the immediate and thorough reaction, Shankman quickly posted an update on his Twitter account, saying "Omni hotels is full of win - They monitor Twitter, and upped the wifi within a half-hour. Well done." This post received even more retweets, with users commending Omni for its progressive approach to customer service. The story was even picked up by several blogs and media outlets, truly turning a black eye in to a textbook example of good customer service.

Due to the 24-hour nature of the hotel industry, Omni uses a team approach to monitor buzz online, a process it has continued to refine.

"There were a few occasions at the beginning when we responded to a post more than once," Kboudi said. "Now at the corporate level, we schedule the responder, although we all monitor during the day. We communicate regularly with the field team, and if they see something that should be responded to by the brand, they notify us. We also cross promote each other's handle, including our PR team, so if there is someone looking for specific info, we will direct them to our subject matter expert."

Kboudi's team is one of the more progressive in the hospitality industry when it comes to social media, but she expects the industry to catch up, saying, "In the next few years, we expect to see the social interactions to increase as more people are connecting via smart phones and have the ability to interact with brands 24/7."

Finally, Kboudi points out that Twitter is not just about addressing problems. "When we see that someone is visiting for a special occasion, looking for a recommendation or just having a rough day, we have the opportunity to create a truly memorable experience for them with a 'surprise and delight' moment," she said.

"Fortunately, [the staff at our properties] understand the power of the social networks and the critical need to address an issue on the spot instead of after the stay," she said.

KEY TAKEAWAYS

✓	Offer your network more than just coupons. Give them value through information about your industry as well as your services.
✓	Be transparent: While not all campaigns will generate buzz, advertising through deceit certainly will.
✓	Promote the positive and address the negative comments, while remembering to lean on your fan base for help.
✓	Set a plan to make sure your networks are fresh and nothing said about your brand slips past you.

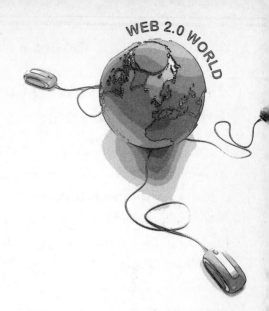

CHAPTER 8

Building Your Network

"He will never have true friends who is afraid of making enemies."

- William Hazlitt, 19th century English philosopher

You know how to monitor the online buzz, how to join the networks, and the ground rules for joining the conversation. Now it is time to build your network. Just like a website is nothing without good search engine optimization to draw in visitors, your social network posts are no good without an audience listening — and it is not always about the size of your network. There are plenty of ways to attract hundreds and even thousands of followers, but finding the right ones is much more important.

Getting followers on Twitter takes a different approach from building your network on LinkedIn, for example. In this chapter, we will look at each of the major platforms to see the best practices for building a strong network of the right people to help you reach your goals online.

Twitter: Interact With Customers, Prospects, and Peers

Twitter became a sensation in 2009, with its monthly unique visitors growing more than 400 percent from January to December, according to Compete (**www.compete.com**). While the other platforms are filled with features, apps, and tools, Twitter is overly simple. Just 140 characters and that is it. This has made it a great platform for people too busy to write a full blog post that still want to stay up on the latest trends. From a business perspective, Twitter can be used to interact with customers, keep an eye on the competition, or monitor news about your industry. Building a strong network is extremely important on Twitter. It is not just about the number of people that follow you, but how many people follow them, and so on. Writing a good post will get it retweeted by others, expanding your reach exponentially. That is why it is so important to focus on the right followers, rather than just trying to reach a specific overall number.

Software might not bring you the right followers

Very soon after joining Twitter, you will inevitably get direct messages from new followers saying something to the effect of "learn how to get hundreds of new followers a day by clicking here." This is tempting, but it is not a great way to build a strong network. One knock on Twitter is that it is comprised of a bunch of people talking with nobody listening. If you go with this type of software, that is exactly what you will find. The people following you are doing so just to build their own networks, and so goes the cycle.

Here is how those programs work. First you give the software your username and password, and in most cases your credit card number. Tweet Adder and Hummingbird, two of the more popular systems, cost $55 and $69.97 respectively. Based on keywords you provide them, they will go out and follow as many people as Twitter allows in a day, which is

1,000. The program will then monitor which of those users follow you back over a period of a couple of days. If someone does not follow you back in that time, the program will unfollow him or her in order to keep your ratio of following to followers even. The person followed does not see how the follower found them, whether it was from a personal search or an automated system.

The main problem with these programs is the message they send. By letting an application choose who you follow, you are admitting that you have no interest in listening to what others have to say. Of course, your goal is to have other people read what you write, but that can only happen when you participate in conversations and build relationships. The result will be tens of thousands of followers for you, with none of them really listening. You are better off building your network organically to have a strong group of people actually interested in what you have to offer them.

Another popular type of tool is one that follows people automatically based on keywords in their tweets. Applications like Twollow will scan new posts on Twitter for the keywords you specify and follow any users that mention them. For example, a company that makes saddles might choose to automatically follow anyone that mentions saddles or horses, usually in hopes of getting followed back by that user. That explains why the next time you tweet about your dry cleaner you will have a handful of dry cleaners follow you almost immediately. These services run anywhere from a few dollars a month to upward of $100 a year.

To some degree, these types of programs have taken away from the authenticity of Twitter. In the past, seeing that someone had 5,000, 50,000, or even 500,000 followers was a good indication that they are a strong resource. While that might be true today, it might also mean they have deep pockets. It will be interesting to see if Twitter continues to allow these types of applications to run on your API as they move closer to a monetization strategy.

CASE STUDY: BUILDING YOUR NETWORK IN ACTION

Kim Wilson, president and cofounder
Play Action Online
(www.playactiononline.com)

When it comes to growing a small business, the simplest approach is not always the best. Kim Wilson, cofounder and president of Play Action Online and creator of the gaming website CampPete.com (www.camp-pete.com), learned that lesson the hard way. Her site is an online virtual world that teaches kids about football, exercise, and healthy living. It features video messages and tutorials from current NFL and former University of Southern California head coach Pete Carroll.

Wilson's team created a custom Twitter application to promote the website. Interns from the local university helped populate the program with sports trivia questions. Originally at Twitter.com/camppete, the program would tweet out one multiple-choice question every hour. Followers would then reply with the letter of the right answer. Correct answers can earn the user points to use within the virtual world.

While the number of followers was growing for the account, Wilson wanted to accelerate the growth. She started by having the company's interns manually follow users tweeting about football or other relevant keywords. After the company's account was briefly suspended, Wilson became aware that she had violated Twitter's limit of 1,000 new follows per day and had to scale things back. According to Twitter's support site, "While there are technical reasons behind having some limit on following activities, this per-day limit exists to discourage spamminess. Also, it is unlikely that anyone can actually read tweets from thousands of accounts, which makes the mass following activity disingenuous."

While the interns were effective, it was not the best use of their time. So Wilson invested in the Tweet Adder software. Between the constant activity from the software and the previous suspension, Twitter ended up disabling the account for good, as shown in Figure 52.

Fig. 52: With the account permanently disabled, CampPete.com was forced to create a new account at twitter.com/PeteCarrollCamp.

"We learned the hard way that those programs do work...they just work too well," Wilson said. "As promised, we followed a lot of people, and they followed back. And that's why we got suspended."

Wilson said she "filed an appeal but never heard anything back. So we had to start over with a completely new handle."

The new account has more than 200 followers but is no longer one of the company's main marketing efforts. Instead, they have invested in its Facebook fan page and acquiring links from popular gaming directories.

Reciprocate requests

The next question to consider is when to follow back those who follow you. Knowing now that many of the people who follow you are only doing so in hopes of a reciprocal follow, it makes the question more difficult to answer. As part of the programs like Tweet Adder, users have the ability to set up their account to auto-follow those that follow them. There are also free programs that do only that. If you do decide to take advantage of them, just keep in mind that you will end up following multilevel marketing scams, pornography websites, and other users you might not follow otherwise. It is a good idea to take a few minutes every few days to purge the questionable companies you have auto-followed.

There are also programs that will automatically send a user a **direct message (DM)** once they follow you. A direct message is like any other tweet except it is only visible to the intended recipient. While an automatic DM is a good way to say thanks for a follow, many people use it to try to drive traffic to their website or get people to sign up for accounts or other services. Remember the importance of building a relationship: Giving someone the hard sell in a meeting is one thing, but you would not do it as you shook his or her hand for the first time.

Another problem with automatic DMs is they can show your insincerity from the beginning. Many people set their automatic DMs to thank someone for a follow and promise that they will follow back. That is fine, but it can look a bit odd when that person is already following you. Things like this and other blunders start your relationship out on the wrong foot and will lead many people to unfollow you right away. A better option might be to send the new follower an @ reply, the term for a tweet that is directed at a specific person but still public, thanking them for the follow. They will likely appreciate your mentioning them to their network. Do not overdo it, though, as your followers do not want to read your thank you notes all day. Consider doing this for specific people or in groups at the end of the day or week.

Consider the cost to follow someone

Following 100 people is pretty easy. If you log in to Twitter or TweetDeck a few times a day, you will be able to keep up with most of what has been said. As you might imagine, that is more difficult when you are following a 1,000 or more people. That is where tools like TweetDeck's columns come in handy, allowing you to segment the people you follow in to different groups, making the content easier to digest at a glance. Inevitably, there are certain people that tweet every second of every day. Some tweet about the mundane things they are doing, letting you know exactly when they eat each meal. Others may be offering great content but just too much of it.

The website follow cost (**www.followcost.com**) has made an amusing yet functional tool to calculate the cost to follow someone in terms of your time. It bases its system on notorious blogger and habitual-tweeter Robert Scoble (@scobleizer). The Microsoft alumni and current Rackspace employee is a celebrity with one of the top 50 most popular technology blogs, according to Technorati. He also tweets all day, every day with more than 33,000 tweets as of April 2010. Follow cost calculates someone's number of tweets in relation to Scoble's, giving it a "milliscoble" rating. If Scoble tweets an average of 21 times a day, then one milliscoble is 0.021. According to the site, shown in Figure 53, a person with an index of 1,000 is "as annoying to follow" as Scoble.

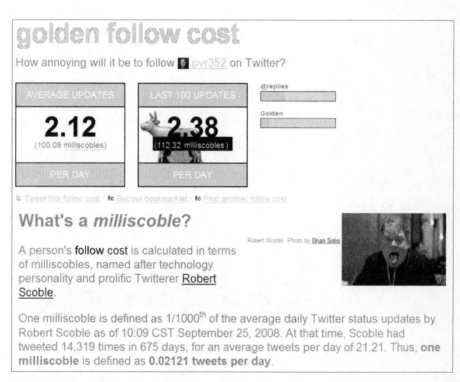

Fig. 53: The milliscoble index is a tongue-in-cheek look at how annoying someone is to follow.

The lesson here is to not overdo it. It obviously has not been an issue for Scoble, with well more than 100,000 followers. However, if you over-tweet before you earn someone's trust, there is a good chance you will lose followers. Nothing is more annoying to a Twitter user to log in and only see posts from one person dominating his or her screen.

Reach out to existing contacts

Many people start looking for new people to follow from day one. However, one of the easiest ways to build your Twitter network is to locate people you already know who are on Twitter. You may find that customers or coworkers are more willing to open up to you in a more casual form like Twitter. After you have created an account, you can allow Twitter to search your address books on your Gmail, Yahoo!, or AOL e-mail accounts, as shown in Figure 54. From this same page, you can invite people to join you on Twitter via e-mail.

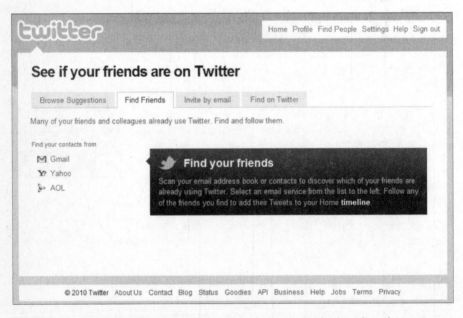

Fig. 54: Connecting with people you already know and who already trust you will help you gain access to their networks.

If you are committed to using Twitter as a resource for your customers and to find new ones, then you should promote it offline as well. Make it easy for other Twitter users to find you by adding your Twitter page to your e-mail signature. Add your corporate account to your website's contact page. If several people are tweeting for your business, list all of their accounts as well. Depending on how heavily you use the service, you might also consider adding it to your business cards.

Search for people talking about your industry

Once you have connected with your existing business contacts, it is time to branch out. Social networks are about interacting with new people, so you need to look outside of your current circle. One of the easiest ways to do that is through a hashtag search. If you have spent some time on Twitter, you have no doubt seen posts with the # symbol followed by a word or acronym.

Say, for example, you are interested in following the buzz around an event like the annual TED (Technology, Education, Design) Conference. While there will, of course, be people who tweet about the event without mentioning the name, many will use a predetermined hashtag the event promotes on its website, like #TED. The actual tag might be promoted by the event organizers or just adopted by the community. What this allows you to do is to search for #TED on Twitter or an application like TweetDeck and immediately see all of the posts that include that tag. While the main conference takes place only once a year, a search will always show the discussion related to recent blog posts or videos posted by the conference organizers.

Taking advantage of hashtags will do more than simply keep you updated on a particular topic. It can also help you find like-minded users you may want to follow. There are hashtags for everything from television shows and sporting events to business events, product launches, and industry news.

Using the power of programs like TweetDeck, you can set up a column to constantly monitor a specific hashtag that interests you, and use that as a way to find new connections.

Another way to find certain types of users on Twitter is through a service like Twellow (**www.twellow.com**), which, unlike Twitter, allows you to search within a user's profile for specific keywords. Twitter's search only looks at users' names or the contents of their tweets. Searching in Twellow will help you find other people in your job or role, others in your industry, or people in your target audience. The search in Figure 55 shows people listed as reporters, sorted by the number of followers. This is partly why a well-written bio can have a powerful influence on growing your reach.

Fig. 55: In addition to your Twitter profile, users can register with Twellow to list an extended bio. This helps you come up in more searches.

Follow people attending events you are attending

Event organizers are becoming more and more likely to encourage attendees to tweet with a specific hashtag when discussing a tradeshow or conference. Some conferences go so far as to display the tweets on monitors throughout the event. This allows other attendees to get a beat on what is popular, like a specific exhibit or seminar, or what to avoid. It is also a good way for companies to promote their booth or arrange impromptu get-togethers for after hours. For those not able to attend the event, following the hashtag lets them stay on top of any announcements as they happen.

In addition to helping you stay connected at an event, you can use the hashtag to find new people to follow. Look for people with tweets you agree with or those posting good information. You might identify people who have a large following online that you did not know about. Get involved with the conversation by replying to their posts and following them. If they see you tweeting about the same event, they may follow you back, building your network with people relevant to your industry.

Locate leaders in your industry

Connecting with industry experts or even celebrities is much easier now because of Twitter than it has been in the past. The vast majority of users, even the biggest names out there, tweet for themselves. Savvy users can typically recognize if someone is using a ghostwriter, and word spreads fast that the user is not genuine. The business implications of this openness can be significant. Having a celebrity or high-profile figure in your business mention your product, something nearly impossible to achieve before Twitter without either plenty of luck or even more money, can now happen easily.

The first step is identifying the right people. When looking at Internet celebrities, there are two types on Twitter: those there solely for self-promotion, and those there to interact with their fans and followers. The easiest way to determine who falls under which category is to look at their ratio of followers to people they are following. If someone has 1 million followers but is only following 25 people, they may be less likely to be interested in what you have to say. This is not a steadfast rule, of course. People like Ashton Kutcher, with more than 4 million followers, could not possibly keep up with following that many back. Instead, he seems to monitor people mentioning him or those tweeting in his area and replies to them personally. Once you identify a person with a more balanced ratio, look at his or her timeline, which lists the latest tweets. If he or she is replying to other users' comments, then he or she is a good target for you.

Start by following the person. That indicates you are interested in interaction and not just getting a plug. Then, wait for a post from them where you can provide a good response. You may try humor to get his or her attention. Other options would be to pose a question or recommend a product or service of yours that might help with what he or she tweeted about. Resist the temptation to reply to every post. Waiting for the right one has a better chance of a reply, and a barrage of replies could be an annoyance if the person actually takes the time to read all of his or her replies. If you are lucky, he or she will reply to your post to thank you for your comment or advice or to respond to your question. That tweet will show up in his or her timeline and will be seen by the user's massive following. That could mean anything from a bump in your following to a bump in sales or Web traffic.

Keep your tweets relevant

Most tweets from businesses consist of a combination of promotional announcements, coupons, links, and commentary on industry news. This is a perfectly acceptable approach and should result in a consistent following. If just acceptable is not enough, there are good ways to create a more involved user base. One constant that we have seen in the Twitter success stories like @DellOutlet and @NakedPIZZA is that each of those accounts promote deals that are exclusive to Twitter. This gives customers an incentive to follow your Twitter account, even if they already connect with you in other places, such as on Facebook or directly on your website. It also gives you a way to directly track the results from your efforts. Remember: NakedPizza's sales from Twitter were so strong that it added a Twitter button to its point-of-sale system for cashiers to record the transactions.

There is a fine line when it comes to tweeting, or using any social network for that matter, between staying on topic and keeping with the theme of the medium. Your goal may be to recruit employees, drum up business, or maintain client relationships. However, your tweets are up against ones linking to funny videos, breaking news, and personal conversations between friends. That is some difficult competition as you vie for your audiences' attention. There is no set formula for your tweet's content, such as one business tweet for every funny one. It is all about finding your own voice. Have fun. If you are more comfortable with a professional tone, stick with it. If your approach is more casual and you want to inject some personal anecdotes, even better. People will look at your tweet history before following you, so whatever approach you take, stick with it. Trying to wedge a coupon code in between two links to viral videos if they are not in the same tone will come across as awkward, and awkward leads to losing followers' attention.

Facebook: Focus on Customers and Prospects

Facebook is currently the big kid on the block, and its numbers are showing no signs of slowing. What started as a site for college kids now hosts more than 400 million people including everyone from grandparents to high school students. And the best part of Facebook from a marketer's perspective is the stranglehold the site has on its members' attention. According to Facebook's website, users spend a staggering average of 55 minutes per day on its site. What started as the wild west for advertising has turned in to a platform that now clearly dictates how companies can interact with individuals through applications, fan pages, and advertising. The result is an active marketplace that requires the attention of your business.

Pages versus profiles, fans versus friends

In the beginning, there were profiles. People had profiles, and so did businesses, even though they were not supposed to according to Facebook's terms of use. The lines were blurred between what constituted an advertisement and what was a real person. Some companies set up profiles for their mascots, accumulating friends just like an individual would. A Gainesville, Florida Ben & Jerry's, for example, set up an account for Woody Cow, a mascot it would send to events to promote the scoop shop. At the same time, other companies were creating "groups," which are small networks within the overall network that people with similar interests can join. Finally, there were "fan pages," which users could set up to interact with other fans of everything from soda brands to sports teams. The result was that companies did not know where they were supposed to be, much less where they needed to be, and their customers could not easily find them if they wanted to.

In late 2009, Facebook officially stepped in and clearly defined who could go where. Profiles were limited to individuals, and thus Woody Cow (with the more than 300 friends he had accumulated) was no more. But businesses were not kicked off the site. Instead, they were given fan pages. This allowed them to set up a different kind of page without all of the profile questions that did not apply to business profiles, like where you went to high school or when you were born. This is just one of the reasons for the change, since these things clearly do not apply to businesses but in some cases were required fields, leading to misinformation on the site.

It is important to note that a new business cannot just go on Facebook and create a fan page. Only an individual, most likely an individual representing that business with an existing personal profile on the site, can do that. Only after you have set up your personal page can you create a fan page. After the fan page is up, you can share administration by setting other fans as co-administers of the fan page. In April 2010, Facebook changed the language from "become a fan" to "like" when referring to the relationship between individuals and businesses, according to Mashable (**www.mashable.com**).

This is helpful in separating your personal information from your business. Many employees were reluctant to become friends with their employers during the time when companies had personal profiles because of the access the company's human resources department or even CEO would have to their personal information like photos and status updates. Under the fan page model, personal information beyond the name and profile picture is not made public to the company after a user becomes a fan. People who want a separation of work and personal relationships can still experience both on Facebook without jeopardizing either. A company does not have the same access to a fan's personal information that they do to a friend's.

The importance of earning fans should not be taken lightly. Earning a customer takes significant time and money. However, the next time that person is ready to buy, you have to earn his or her business again, either through new advertising or a positive buying experience. Once people become fans on Facebook, they remain fans unless they actively go into their profiles to change that. This gives you indefinite, direct access to qualified clients or leads.

Filtering out the noise

For all the great things about Facebook, there are some potential annoyances, specifically if you are planning to use it primarily for your business. During your registration, you set things like where you went to high school and college. As a result of being listed in those networks, you will find all sorts of people you were not great friends with in the past wanting to "reconnect." There is no harm in making these connections, especially because you want your profile to look personal and not like a billboard, even if you do only use it for business. Plus, you never know: That person who sat behind you in math class might work for your biggest customer.

As alluded to in Chapter 6, Facebook now allows you to categorize friends into groups, setting different levels of access to different groups. For example, you might create a group for coworkers, business contacts, family members, old school friends, and then the people you actually socialize with. Then, you can select to hide your pictures from your business contacts and coworkers. By targeting your profile around these groups, you are encouraging the right kinds of interaction with each subset.

Regardless of how you set up your profile, there will always be unwanted requests. While you are using Facebook as a marketing tool, millions of others are using it as a place to unwind. That means invitations to play games or share other applications like movie quizzes and personality tests. Remember chain letters? They are back, but now without all the stamps and envelopes. All of these requests, along with the legitimate ones you may be interested in, are displayed on one notifications page. *Take a look back at Figure 41 in Chapter 6 for a refresher in blocking out the applications that can quickly clutter your inbox.* Also, setting your notifications to your preferences will ensure the frivolous applications do not ever make it to your email.

Many people are concerned about offending someone by hitting the ignore button for event or fan page requests, as well as general friend requests. Facebook has designed the process to be non-confrontational. After someone adds you as a friend, he or she will see a note next to your name when he or she looks at your public profile that says "awaiting friend confirmation." If you choose not to accept the request, that person does not get a notice saying you do not like them. The only change is instead of saying "awaiting friend confirmation," the other user will once again see "add as friend." There are no options under Facebook's notifications for a person to be e-mailed when you deny his or her request.

Take advantage of the events feature

Facebook's events feature is a great way to not only promote a specific event but also to expand your network. Events within Facebook are basically online invitations. You can input all of the who, what, and where information and also add photos and notes. You can invite people from your network, including specific categories you may have set up. Depending on their notification preferences, they will receive an e-mail or a notice the next time they login to the site. The event page shows who is attending and who is not, as well as who has yet to reply. But here is where it gets interesting. When creating the event, you can elect to let invitees forward the invitation to their network, as shown in Figure 56. They can also share the event on their profile, helping your message extend well beyond your contacts. Make sure to monitor the list of RSVPs, adding those people you do not already know to your list of friends.

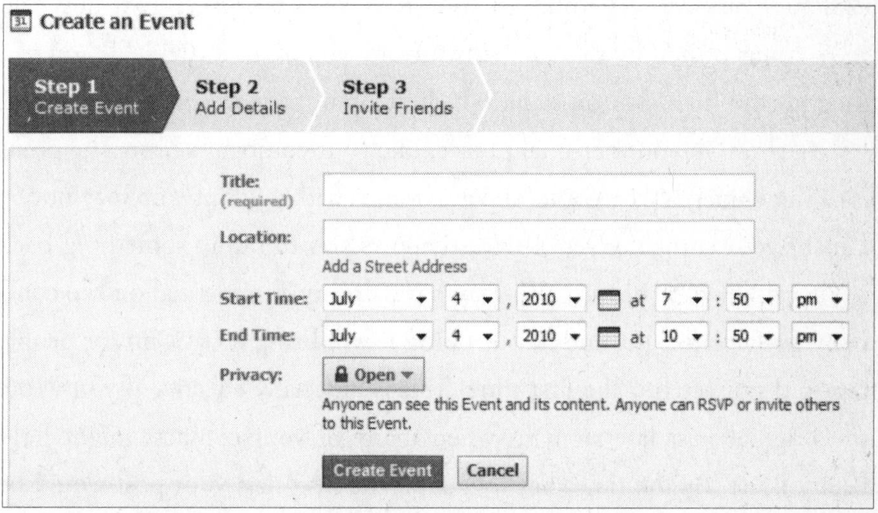

Fig. 56: Make sure to leave your event as "Open" in the privacy settings if you want users to share it with their network.

"Like" and comment on company info

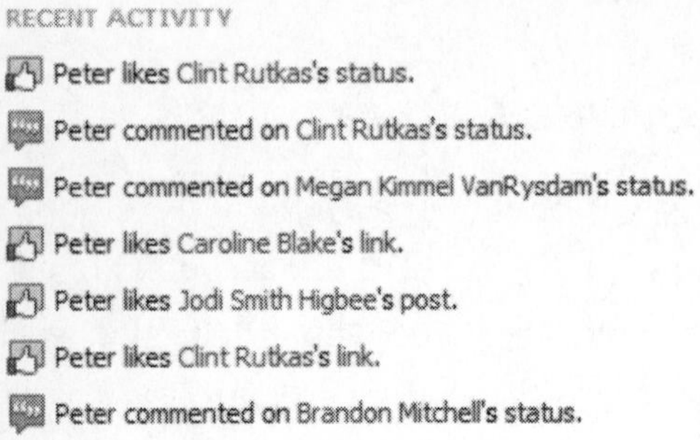

RECENT ACTIVITY

Peter likes Clint Rutkas's status.

Peter commented on Clint Rutkas's status.

Peter commented on Megan Kimmel VanRysdam's status.

Peter likes Caroline Blake's link.

Peter likes Jodi Smith Higbee's post.

Peter likes Clint Rutkas's link.

Peter commented on Brandon Mitchell's status.

Fig. 57: "Likes" show up in a user's recent activity, along with a link to whatever post it relates to.

When you like something, you tend to share that with your friends. Facebook has made this inclination easier by adding a "like" button to virtually like anything from users' status updates and pictures. One of your goals is to have people "like" your posts, and not just because of the warm feeling of acceptance you will feel inside. When someone "likes" something on Facebook, it shows up on their profile in the recent activity section, like the example in Figure 57. The more "likes," the more exposure your link, update, or picture receives outside of your network.

You can also use the "like" feature to promote your own posts. Say for example you post something to your company's fan page. That post will show up as posted by the company, not by you as an individual. You can then hit the "like" button to have it show up in your recent activity. It will say that you, in your personal profile, like your company's post. The point is to show the post to people who are friends with you but who may not be fans of your company yet. This also allows you to bump something back to the top of your profile. You may have already commented on the company update after posting it, but liking it will bring it back up for people that did not catch it the first time. This is especially effective if you wrote the original post late at night when many of your contacts might have been offline. By the time they logged in the next day, your post would be buried under other updates. Liking it at a different time of day gets it seen by more people. Determining the best time is specific to your business. A

B2B company should try to post things during business hours, while B2C companies may want to focus on evenings and weekends.

Commenting on status updates, links, or photos can have the same effect as the "like" feature. In addition to commenting on your company's updates to promote them to your network, consider commenting on other active topics. Under the default notification settings, you will receive e-mail updates if other users comment on something you also commented on. That means if you comment on a post that ten other people have all commented on, chances are they will each get an e-mail, regardless of whether you are friends with them. This is another great way to get your name in front of other users.

Facebook "connect" and custom apps

Just as Twitter allows users to use the service outside of their websites, Facebook does, too. However Facebook keeps a little tighter grip on the reigns, due in large part to the greater amount of personal identifiable information it stores on its users versus Twitter. Web developers can use a service called Facebook Connect to integrate certain functionality into their own websites. The most basic application of Facebook Connect is allowing users to share a picture, blog post, or other piece of content to their wall from your site without ever leaving your page. Not only does this encourage your visitors to promote your content on social networks, but it also keeps the user on your site. If you were to simply link them to Facebook, you might have a tough time getting their attention back.

Facebook Connect implementations can go much further than simply sharing a link. Users can comment, share rich content like Flash or multimedia, or be served targeted content based on their Facebook profiles. More and more sites are also using Facebook as a way to have users sign into their websites. For example, many blogs now allow users to post comments using their Facebook ID rather than create an account, a feature Facebook says could increase registrations by as much as 300 percent on some sites. The popular news aggregator Digg uses this feature to make the user experience simpler on its website.

Fig. 58: Ben and Jerry's website lets users rate and become a fan of a particular flavor without leaving their site. The interactions are posted to the users' wall for all of their friends to see.

Allowing users to share things between your website and their Facebook account can be a very powerful tool. First off, it gets your message in front of a wider audience. It can go beyond that to help keep your brand on top of the original user's mind. Take a flooring store, for example. Most flooring websites allow you to look at sample, and some even allow you to specify things like your paint or fabric colors to see how they look against the carpet, tile, or wood options. That is already a rich user experience, but one can go much further by adding Facebook Connect. Once a user picks his or her favorite, Facebook Connect would allow them to post it to his or her wall along with a comment, perhaps asking friends for their opinion on the color choice. This example takes a great experience and makes it that much better by engaging not only the original customer but also potentially hundreds of other prospects. Ben and Jerry's has done something similar, as shown in Figure 58, by allowing users to comment on and become a fan of its ice cream flavors using Facebook Connect.

The basic functions of Facebook Connect are relatively simple for a Web developer to integrate on a site. Depending on the specifics, it may be as little as a couple of hours of a developer's time. More advanced installations could cost thousands or even tens of thousands of dollars. However, the return on investment should also go up with a more feature-rich website because a richer experience should encourage more customer interaction and sharing.

Companies have also profited from Facebook by creating applications, or apps, that live within their Facebook fan page. Apps go beyond the simple fan page to provide users with a more interactive and customized experience. By accepting an app's terms of use, companies get a more complete look at the demographic information about their users. In addition to earning more fans, one of the main goals of most companies creating an app is to get access to more information about their customers. Apps can be complex, and costly, like interactive games designed to hold a customer's attention, or they can be as simple as a form that gathers information in exchange for a promotion.

CASE STUDY: FACEBOOK APPS IN ACTION

Pete Zimek, owner
The Caffeine Bar at Ben & Jerry's
(www.facebook.com/caffeinebar)

In January 2010, Gainesville, Florida's local Ben & Jerry's franchise reopened after a week of renovation as The Caffeine Bar at Ben & Jerry's. In addition to selling the company's iconic ice cream flavors, owner Pete Zimek wanted to tap into the coffee and specialty drink market. The idea was to create a bar-like atmosphere that appealed to the town's large crowd of college students. That meant new paint, new seating, and a host of new menu items bringing together ice cream and espresso.

The store has a good customer base but needed a way to get the word out about the changes. Rather than spend the budget on expensive radio or television ads, Zimek and his partners decided to go where his customers were: Facebook.

They started by holding a Vermonster eating contest at their store to raise money for student groups, while also raising awareness for the store. (The Vermonster is Ben & Jerry's mega sundae, with 20 scoops of ice cream and ladles of toppings totaling more than 14,000 calories). The store asked that all the contestants post about the event at least twice beforehand in order to bring in more people. After the event, it posted several pictures and videos about the event that brought in even more buzz. The next step was to create an application on Facebook's platform.

"We hired a developer experienced in creating Facebook campaigns to develop a simple app for us," Zimek said. "Our goal was to build our fan base on the site without spending too much money."

The Facebook page for the Gainesville store was starting from scratch with zero fans in January, which provided a simple benchmark for evaluation of the application's return on investment. The app was a basic form with a branded design, shown in Figure 59, which asked users to become a fan in exchange for a free cone coupon. In order to tap into the social aspect of the website, it also offered a free Javarita, one of the new specialty drinks, to anyone who shared the page with his or her network.

Fig. 59: A local Ben and Jerry's franchise in Gainesville, Florida asks users to become a fan and give some basic information in exchange for a free cone coupon.

The results were surprising, even to Zimek. "We hit 1,500 followers in just over two weeks running the campaign," he said. "Our only expenses were the app itself and under $100 in Facebook advertising to promote the app."

Not only does the store now have new fans it can interact with on Facebook, it also has a host of other information about its customers. By creating an app, the store was able to capture additional demographic information about the new fans, including their names, ages, and e-mail addresses that the store can use in future campaigns. It also asked whether the person had visited the store before, as well as his or her favorite flavor. This is all valuable information the store can use to do things like modify the flavors it stocks.

"Having the new fans is great," Zimek said. "Knowing all the information about them is even better. That is really the most powerful part of the app for us."

Join groups and get involved

One of the simplest ways to build your network is to find groups to join. You might choose to find groups of other people in your industry or job role for professional networking. If there are groups made up of your customers or potential customers, feel free to join them as well. Say you own a home painting company. Depending on your business model, you may want to join groups of builders and remodelers in your region. As a complimentary service, you can try to build relationships with people who may need your services. However, remember the unwritten rules of social media, and do not take that access as a green light to spam the group with advertising. Instead, you should engage other group members in conversations. Once you have made those connections, add those users as friends. Then, only after they have accepted your request should you invite them to become fans of your company.

Advertise your page through PPC ads

The secret is out about pay-per-click advertising: It is a great tool to get your link in front of customers as they are searching to make a purchase. The search engines let you target specific keywords with specific ads in order to hit different users at different stages in the buying process. Facebook offers the same type of advertising model, but with all of the personal information it has on its users, it is able to offer marketers much more targeted ads. Targeting not only gives you the peace of mind that your message is reaching the right people, but you also know you are not paying for clicks from non-qualified users.

To really show off the power of this tool, we need to look at a very specific example using a fictitious small business that provides human resources services to other small businesses in and around Seattle, Washington. Its buyers are usually human resources managers or, with smaller companies, the CEO or owner. As you can see in Figure 60, you can specify the geographical target by city, state, or country. You can target specific age groups, and most important, in this example, the users' likes and interests. For most users, this is where they put their job title. By adding those job roles, we reduced the number of people who will see the ad from more than 2,000,000 to 2,760. In a traditional advertising model, this may be looked at as a bad thing. However, why would you pay for views or clicks from people not interested in your product or who lack the buying power at their company? At the same time, the right users are much more likely to click on your ad if it resonates with a need they have.

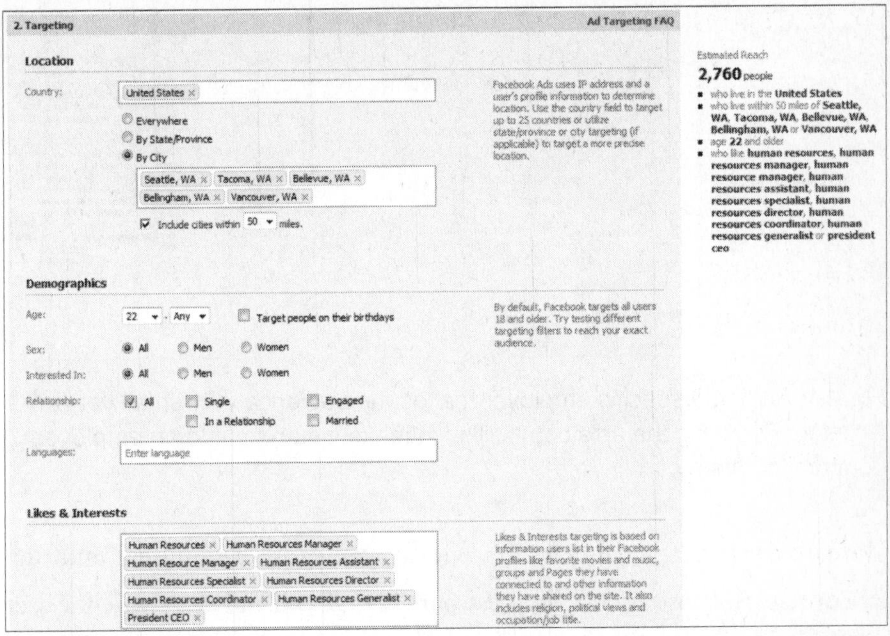

Fig. 60: As you drill down your search on Facebook ads, you are shown a real-time count of the number of users that fit your criteria.

For anyone that has used a service like Google AdWords, you can really appreciate the power this kind of information gives you as an advertiser. However, the location, age, and job role are just the beginning. Staying with the human resources company example, let us assume that they have been trying to get in with one of Seattle's largest companies, Boeing, with no luck. Facebook lets you limit your ad to employees of that company, not by adding terms like airplane to the interests, but by choosing that company from the list of networks. Figure 61 shows that adding Boeing to the employer field brings the reach down to 80 people. Again, you are reducing the number of people who will see your ad, but all you are getting rid of are people who do not work at the company. These people, while they may be fans of Boeing, will not help you earn the business. All they will do is waste your money by clicking on your ad.

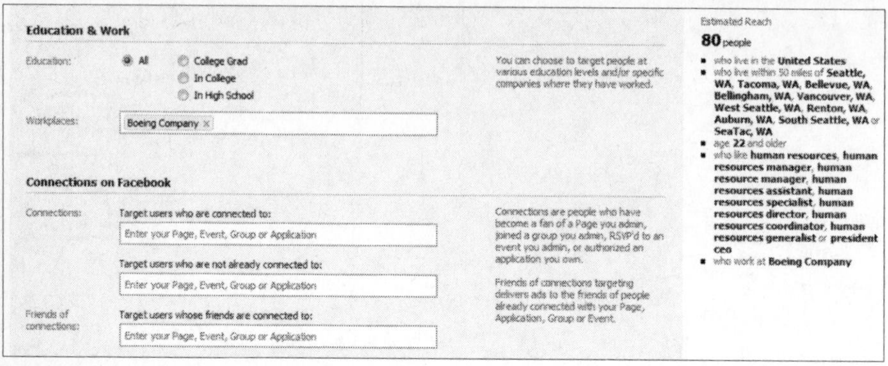

Fig. 61: Adding a specific employer makes the audience very small yet very targeted. Focusing the ad's copy will also make it stand out to an employee from that company.

With an ad that targeted demographically, you can feel confident tailoring its content to those users. The best part is that you only pay when a user clicks on the ad. You can choose to pay for a certain number of impressions, or times, the ad is displayed, but that does not make much sense in this scenario. If you pay by the click, your ad will still be shown to users multiple times, but at no cost to you unless they take action. Rather than have 1,000 people who may or may not be potential customers see an ad once, a very targeted group of qualified leads would see your ad every time they log on the site. In this specific example, Facebook recommends bidding $.46 to $.59 per click, information it provided during the ad generation process. That means that your ad could be shown thousands of times to these 80 users, thus increasing your brand recognition. And all it takes is one click, which costs you less than a latte, for you to get in touch with your white whale — your much sought-after target demographic.

At 352 Media Group, we used Facebook ads for three main goals: to promote awareness to marketing executives responsible for Web development purchases, to recruit students for our internship program, and to reach additional decision makers within one of our largest clients. For the campaign, we wanted to let marketers in departments we had not been introduced to know we were not only an approved vendor, but we were also up to speed on their latest design tool, Microsoft® Silverlight®.

Using Facebook's service, we were able to target college-educated people living in or around Microsoft's campus outside near Seattle. We also specified that we wanted people who worked at Microsoft and had a specific job title. Microsoft marketers are called anything from product managers to product evangelists, and by using these keywords, we were able to hone in on the exact people we wanted to reach. By limiting the audience, we also knew we could use acronyms and terminology specific to Microsoft. Not only would that let us fit our message into Facebook's limited advertising criteria, but we also hoped it would stick out as unique to Microsoft employees.

Within two days of starting the campaign, one of the marketers we had worked with in the past but had lost touch with e-mailed me a screenshot of his Facebook profile with the add on the left. The e-mail simply said, "Cool!" I knew from the statistics Facebook provided us that, despite the small audience, the ad was served up thousands of times and clicked on quite a bit, which helped us extend our reach and build upon an already valuable relationship.

You can create as many different ads as you want, including multiple ads to the same specific target. This gives you the ability to experiment with different titles, graphics, and ad copy to find the combination that earns you the best response. The site's reporting engine shows you the number of impressions, the click-through rate, the average cost per click, and the total amount spent over the time period selected. And, to make sure you do not spend more than you are comfortable with, you can set a daily budget for each ad.

LinkedIn: Professional Networking at its Best

LinkedIn, while the smallest of the major networks featured so far in terms of monthly unique visits, is the most targeted. The site is aimed specifically at business people looking to interact with other business people. In addition to using the site to drum up business, many use the site as a resource when looking for jobs or internships. Not only can users post resumes and search openings, but they can also research a potential employer through the site.

Join all relevant networks to be found

LinkedIn is all about strengthening relationships with people online who you have an existing relationship with offline. Therefore, it is important to make sure you find all of your contacts. As you set up your profile, you will be asked to indicate where you work, including both current and past positions. You will also be able to list your school. This information is used to put you in those networks. Then, for example, you can browse other alumni from your college to make connections. The more connections you have, the more people you can be introduced to outside of your circle. And that means more people to interact, and potentially do business, with. It is no secret that people like to do business with people they trust, and LinkedIn is a great way to meet new people and build that confidence.

Import your contacts

Connecting with other users is not as easy on LinkedIn as it is with other social networks. This is by design, as they want to limit the number of unsolicited e-mails and notifications within the system. The thinking is that more busy executives will join if they know they will not be badgered by spammers. LinkedIn does this by limiting your ability to message people outside of your existing network. You can request to add someone you do not know personally to your network, but if they respond that they do not know you, you will have to enter users' e-mail addresses to make connections in the future.

The best way to build your network is through your existing contacts. LinkedIn lets you import your address book from most e-mail services. It will then locate those users' profiles, allowing you to connect on the site. From there, you can see your contacts' acquaintances, called second-degree contacts. You can request one of your first-degree contacts introduce you to people in their lists, which is more reputable than a random request.

Join industry groups

Like Facebook, LinkedIn uses groups as a way for like-minded people to interact. This might include industry groups, professional associations, or alumni of a particular school or class. Groups encourage users to interact by sharing ideas and asking questions. On a website where your interactions with those outside of your contacts are limited, groups are a great opportunity to meet new people and grow your network. If there is not a relevant group related to your industry or products, you can create one. This allows you to promote yourself and your company in an indirect way.

Get involved in Q&A

While many people use LinkedIn to find clients or vendors, it is also a great forum for sharing information among peers. The website's question and answer feature is the easiest form for this type of communication. Users can post questions about anything from how to deduct certain business expenses to dealing with human resources issues. Anyone, including those outside your network, can post a response. Responses can be private to the person asking the question or can be posted publically to help you get additional exposure. But keep your answers on point; other users can report your answer as spam or as self-promotion. The person who originally posted the question selects the best answer, which is then moved to the top. Users can click to see other questions or answers you have posted as well.

The power of recommendations

A good reference letter can go a long way toward landing a job or earning a new client. LinkedIn makes the recommendation process easier by allowing users to request endorsements on the site. Once written, the reference is included on the user's main profile page. Based on that, writing a reference for a vendor or former coworker is a good way to get your name in front of others who are looking at their profile. Something that takes just a few minutes to write can help you meet new business connections.

Take advantage of the apps

Facebook is full of apps, with everything from games to stock trackers to to-do lists. Twitter's API allows for plenty of apps as well. While LinkedIn does not have nearly the amount of apps as the other sites, it does have some powerful tools. Some of the apps include an Amazon widget that lets users share which business books they are currently reading, a WordPress plug-in that brings in your content if you have a blog on its system, and a tool called TripIt that lets users post their business trips in order to connect with others that are also traveling to the same place.

There are a couple of apps in particular that stand out as more popular features on LinkedIn. The first is Company Buzz. Like some of the social monitoring tools discussed in earlier chapters, Company Buzz keeps tabs on what people are saying about your brand or company specifically on LinkedIn by searching for your name. Since certain things on the network are hidden behind a password, Company Buzz is a good way to see things other monitoring tools might miss. A second app that has gained steam on LinkedIn is SlideShare, an app from the makers of the website by the same name that allows users to upload and share documents and presentations.

The SlideShare app integrates this tool into your profile. That means you can share marketing materials and other information with people in your network. This is a great way to get more mileage out of your hard work. For example, you might have created a presentation for a meeting that you feel would benefit others in your network. Posting it will help others learn about the topic while also helping you build awareness and expert standing on the subject.

Get Everyone Involved: Defining Roles Within Your Company

Starting at the top, the CEO, president, or owner of your company is the best person to be involved in social media. In many small businesses, the person in charge of marketing is also the CEO, so you will need to juggle these duties along with those you will read about in the next few paragraphs. While the message might be the same coming from anyone, there is no doubt the CEO's voice carries more weight. You probably have seen the impact whenever the owner makes an appearance in a sales meeting. People want to connect with those at the top of the ladder who have the most influence.

When it comes to social networks, there are several ways for the CEO to get involved. Chances are his or her (or your) time is limited, so you should approach the boss with a plan that gives your company's social presence a big boost without a large time investment. Or, if you are the owner of your small business, then you should use these tips to create your plan of attack. The best approach is to set a schedule. If you simply get to it when you get to it, it will inevitably get pushed to the bottom of the to do list. The CEO should leave the monitoring to the rest of the team and focus on providing content.

Set a time — the beginning of the week, for example — for the CEO to write a new blog post. Adding this to the calendar will make sure it gets done. Topic ideas will come up during the week, so ask the CEO to keep a list of topics that are current and interesting. Most CEOs do a good bit of reading about their industry in trade publications and websites. This is a great opportunity to create content for other services outside your blog. Adding just two minutes to that part of their day to tweet a link and comment about the most interesting article can go a long way, especially if you have set up tools to propagate the tweets to Facebook, LinkedIn, and any other relevant networks.

Other company executives should follow the same approach, tweeting interesting things as they come across them and blogging on a regular basis. The CEO's job in this scenario is to give the customer a window inside the company. However, others in the company with more time should also consider connecting with their counterparts at other businesses. Marketers are sharing feedback on promotional strategies online, CFOs are sharing accounting ideas, and sales directors may even be sharing leads. Connecting with people beyond your industry is a good way to find unique ideas, as they are more likely to be more candid than your competitors.

The marketing department has a few more responsibilities in keeping up with social networks. While others within the company should just focus on their own accounts, the marketing team — or with many small businesses, the marketing person — should be in charge of any corporate accounts. This includes retweeting good posts from others in the company, updating events on Facebook, uploading multimedia content, and most importantly, monitoring the chatter. Just remember that even though you are representing the company, you should have a personality.

KEY TAKEAWAYS

✓	Grow your networks organically, as this will help you connect with others looking to establish real connections.
✓	While social networks are a great way to discover new people, you should also connect with people already in your Rolodex.
✓	Use Facebook's features like "share" and "like" to keep your content on top of mind and on top of your customers' pages.
✓	Encourage everyone in your company to get involved in social networking, from the top down.

CHAPTER 9

Establish Yourself as an Expert Online

"Never become so much of an expert that you stop gaining expertise. View life as a continuous learning experience."

- Denis Waitley, author of *The Psychology of Winning*

When experts talk, people listen — but what makes an expert? People will listen to anchors and analysts on the news merely because they are on TV; most people do not look at the résumé of a newspaper article's author. Certain degrees or certifications mean someone knows more about a topic than the average person, but that does not make them an expert compared to others in his or her field. Most professions do not have criteria for determining an expert. Take someone like television personality Cesar Millan of The Dog Whisperer. According to his website (**www.cesarsway.com**), he learned his craft through years of practice. He does not have a license or degree that qualifies him as a dog trainer, but he is accepted as one of the top experts in the field because of the way he has positioned himself.

This is also a problem within industries that do have certification processes. Every contractor has the same basic license, and every lawyer takes the same exams, albeit specific to his or her state. And then there are the businesses that do not require a particular certification. There is no test to start a restaurant, no exam required to open a bridal shop, and no governing body that makes someone a graphic designer. Some people undergo years of training for design, though there is nothing stopping anyone else from calling himself or herself a graphic designer. In these fields, the differentiator is work history and experience.

However, within all of these industries, there are experts. There are people the media calls when they need a source on a topic; there are people whose blogs are read by thousands of others looking for insight into an industry. Find a way to become one of those people, and you will expose your business to people who will trust your opinion more than they would if you said the same thing in an advertisement.

The Benefits of Expert Status

Being an expert in your industry is an indirect form of marketing. It will be taxing on your time, and the benefits to your business are not always clear. You may be asked to participate in speaking engagements, write articles, be interviewed, and more. But every time you get in front of people as an expert, the things you say and the examples you show are no longer viewed as sales pitches. You become more than just an employee of a company but a person with insight who just happens to work for that company. And when people are done coming to you for advice, they will come to you to do business. Besides, everyone wants to do business with the best.

A simple search in Twellow for the term "social media expert" will yield more than 1,000 bios of people claiming to be experts. Unfortunately for you, the term gets thrown around too much. Social media experts are just one example, but this is something that exists in virtually every industry. Just declaring yourself an expert is not enough. Instead, you need to establish yourself as such through your actions. You cannot simply take your company's marketing presentations and pass them off as unbiased information. Instead, you need to actually provide informative, relevant, and impartial content that people will want to share. This chapter will look at a few of the ways you can make that happen.

The Power of Video

The example used earlier about TV anchors is especially interesting with today's technology. Thanks to sites like YouTube, everyone with a camcorder or webcam has the ability to reach just as many people as a television host does. In many cases, viral sensations have reached much farther. YouTube has done to television what blogs have done to newspapers and magazines: It has given the average citizen an equal voice unmatched in history. But unlike TV, the viewer controls the online video. They hold the power to watch whatever they want, whenever they want.

The kneejerk reaction for companies was to put their television-style commercials online when YouTube and other sites first grabbed viewers' attention. However, if users were already fast-forwarding through commercials on their TV's digital video recorders, they were not about to start watching them online. Then businesses saw the need to create amazing, unique, or — in some cases — simply absurd videos often unrelated to their message with the hopes of the video going viral. This proved an effective approach for many companies. In response, advertising agencies began producing videos that were clearly staged or doctored, hoping to cash in on this trend.

You cannot force viral

CiCi's Pizza had success in terms of building buzz and awareness with a video of a man twirling a sign advertising its pizza buffet then doing a back flip off of a moving bus. Nike had Kobe Bryant jump over a speeding car, seen in Figure 62. The NFL and Reebok had players perform increasingly unbelievable stunts from catching a football through a sheet of drywall to jumping from one side of an SUV to another through its opened windows.

All of these videos had tens of thousands of viewers. At the same time, along with countless other examples, they made the public skeptical about videos that seemed too good to be true. Trying to create that style video today with the hope it will become a viral hit requires a Hollywood production team and a matching budget.

Fig. 62: Basketball star Kobe Bryant shown jumping a speeding car in a YouTube.com video. The video opens with Kobe showing his Nike sneakers to the camera.

While you may get lucky and create something people just have to share, you may be better off focusing on quality views rather than the quantity. Video is inherently more engaging than text, so consider turning things you would normally write into videos. This might include training sessions for existing clients or product demos for prospects. Case studies can be more interesting in video form, especially if you can interview your customers to let them share their success stories. And while the absurd and over-the-top videos might not have the broad reach due to the massive amount of similar content available, they can still be a good way to show your staff's personalities. They may even be good recruiting tools.

Selecting the right video tools

While televisions continue to get bigger screens requiring a super-crisp picture, the expectation is not nearly as high online. Some of the most iconic videos ever to hit YouTube were shot from a laptop's built-in webcam, and that is good news for your budget. For things like product tours, a basic webcam with a built-in microphone or even an inexpensive digital video camera will more than suffice. Quality webcams run anywhere from $20 to more than $100, while several models of handheld digital video cameras with built-in USB connections or removable memory cards are less than $200 and interface directly with sites like YouTube. Either one is a good option since they do not require transferring video from tapes.

If your video will feature a website or software program, you should get a screen-recording program. With these tools, you specify the area or specific window you want to record, and the software will capture every click, mouse movement, and animation that happens on your screen. An adequate free tool is AutoScreenRecorder, shown in Figure 63, available for download from **http://wisdom-soft.com**, which also offers a paid version with a few more bells and whistles. One of the most popular products is Camtasia, which offers a free 30-day trial at TechSmith (**www.techsmith.com/camtasia**). Both products will let you export the video into several popular formats like .wmv or .avi, and Camtasia even includes some good editing functionality that lets you import voice narration and text overlays.

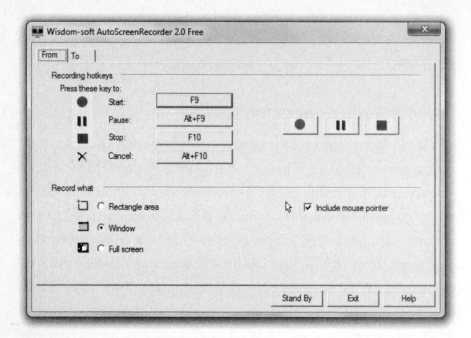

Fig. 63: The free screen recorder from Wisdom-soft provides the basic features needed to capture Web quality video.

If you are looking for something a little fancier, you can create a basic studio for less than $500. TubeTape (**www.tubetape.com**) has packages that include lights, a green screen background with a stand, and basic editing software at that price point. With a little practice, you can remove the background and replace it with anything from your logo to a virtual set. This is a great option if you are looking to produce a video blog or other recurring show that is going to require more than just a point-and-shoot camera. The bottom line is Web video does not have to cost as much as you might think.

Once you have your equipment, you can start producing content right away. The rules of Web video are a bit different than what you see on television. The first thing to consider is the length of your video. Do not take five minutes to say something you can get across in two. With so many choices of things to watch, users simply do not have the attention span to sit through a lengthy video. Studies suggest users tend to drop off during longer videos, with video marketing company Wistia (**http://wistia.com/ blog**) finding the average viewer watched 85 percent of a 30 second video, and only 50 percent of a two minute video.

What is especially interesting about that study was that both videos used the exact same content for the first 30 seconds. At the 30 second mark, just under 50 percent of viewers were still watching the shorter video while only 25 percent were still tuned in to the longer one. This confirms the suspicion that people are less likely to commit to longer videos. The research also showed that, while there was a significant difference between the 30-second and two-minute video, there was little drop-off between the two-minute video and videos up to 10 minutes. That suggests that while videos under two minutes will hold the average user's attention for more time, there is no real reason to try to push an eight-minute video down to five minutes. If you can get them past the two-minute mark, chances are you have a user committed to that video.

Once your video is shot and edited, it is time to put it online. While You-Tube is not the only player in town, it is certainly the biggest. What that means is that there is a better chance of someone finding your video through its search as a related video from another one on a similar topic. Be careful when setting up your account, as your username will also be part of the Web address to your channel. This channel, which is basically a list of all of your uploads, can be customized to include your logo and color scheme.

When you upload a video, use the same tips for writing your website's content when coming up with the description. YouTube's viewing statistics will show you what keywords people used to find your video, which can help you when you write future titles and descriptions. You can also embed the video on your website or blog by pasting the code they provide into your site's HTML. A third way to bring in viewers is to associate your video with a popular existing video, making sure you choose one that is not competitive. Say you are uploading a video about choosing a mortgage for your lending company. Find a video about a complementary topic like home-buying tips or new construction in the search, and then list your video as a response by clicking the link below that video. The other user will need to approve the link, but assuming he or she does, your video will show up underneath the popular one as a video response.

There are certain situations, like a video of a speaking event or seminar, where a longer recording is justified. However, YouTube limits an upload's length to 10 minutes, so you will need to look into other channels for particularly long segments. Blip.tv (**http://blip.tv**) offers a very similar service and supports clips more than an hour long. You can still embed the video elsewhere and access viewing statistics, making it a good alternative when your video just will not fit in less than ten minutes.

Webinars: Advertising in Disguise

Nowadays, few people would volunteer to sit through a day of sales pitches, much less pay to attend them. At the same time, business people are shelling out thousands of dollars to attend seminars and conferences. While speaking at these kinds of events is a great way to promote yourself as an industry expert, it is not an easy place to start, especially if you are a small business owner. Popular conferences may receive hundreds of speaker submissions, and they will often select presenters representing brands with a household name. Webinars, on the other hand, are a great way to promote yourself and your company; they can also be a stepping-stone toward live speaking opportunities.

Before the presentation

A webinar is exactly what it sounds like: a Web seminar. Just like a live conference session, webinars usually consist of a presentation with slides, videos, or other content as well as a question-and-answer session with the audience. Some software tools even let you conduct impromptu polls of the audience during the session. There are several comparable webinar platforms available, including GoToWebinar.com, ReadyTalk.com, Webex. com, and Adobe's Connect. Some, like Connect, charge per user, while others charge a flat rate per webinar or per month.

Choosing a topic for your webinar is an important decision. You may decide to speak on a general topic with broad appeal or to focus in on a specific thing that may bring in a smaller, yet more engaged, audience. Whatever you decide, make sure the content is not a sales pitch. In fact, your company should only be included as a supporting role to the webinar's topic. For example, you could say that your company presents the webinar, but remember that no one will volunteer to sit through your sales pitch. If they did, you would not have a job. The user needs to see a tangible benefit from attending; they need to know they are going to learn something. Your company's name can be included during your introduction, through case studies, and with links at the end; however, it should never be the focus of the presentation.

All of the strategies you have learned so far to promote your business can also be used to advertise the webinar. And since you are offering a free service rather than a product, you may even see better response rates. Once you have set up the webinar, start by writing a blog post about it, linking to the registration page. From there, you should tweet about it, post it on Facebook and LinkedIn, and even write a press release to include on your website. Encourage your family, friends, coworkers, and colleagues to retweet the announcement. You may want to go so far as to invite all of your active leads — and do not overlook existing clients. A webinar might be just what you need to revive the relationship with someone who has done business with you in the past but may not know about your latest offerings. In addition to these tactics, there are also free services available specifically for the promotion of webinars. EventSpan (**www.eventspan. com**) is a free website that lists upcoming webinars by date and topic.

People are always looking for fresh ideas or information about confusing topics, so use relevant keywords in your submission to make sure your prospects find your listing.

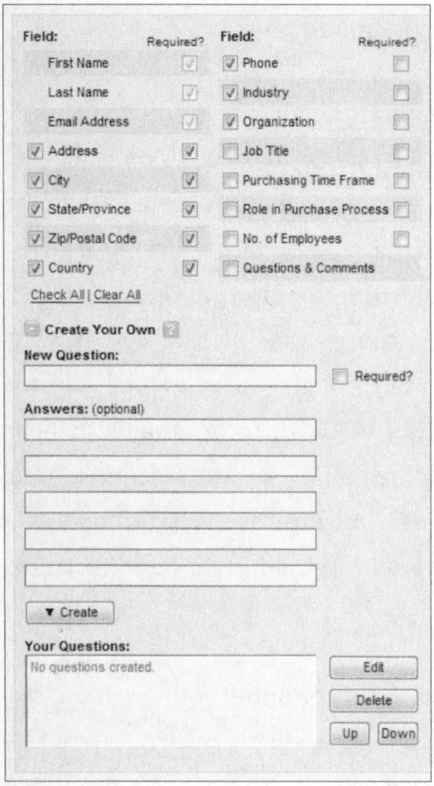

Fig. 64: Creating custom questions through a platform like GoToWebinar's shown here will help you tailor your presentation based on the attendee's goals.

Each new attendee registration for your event is great for two reasons. First and foremost, you will have another person listening to your presentation. In addition, the registration process itself gives you a great opportunity to gather some important and very useful information from the registrant. Each webinar platform will have different options, but most allow you to ask custom questions, such as what the user is hoping to get out of the session, if they already use a product or services like yours, or any other information you want to know. You can also grab some basic contact information, like in the GoToWebinar (**www.gotomeeting. com/fec/webina**r) interface shown in Figure 64. However do not take advantage of the situation and go overboard with your questions. For example, ask yourself if you really need the person's fax number. You may lose out on a possible lead if an overly complicated form frustrates the user. Instead, use the registration to add new people to your database and get insight into what you need to present to satisfy your users.

Practice makes perfect

There is one more step that comes before you host your first Webinar, and that is to practice. Many of the software tools on Webinar platforms allow you to run through a test session. This is an important step in the process for several reasons. First, you can work out any technical concerns. Having someone else from your organization watch your practice event from another computer will ensure your users only see the parts of your screen you intend. You can also use this session to test the audio. When doing this, keep in mind that some services let users choose how to listen. People with higher-speed Internet connections may prefer to listen on their computer speakers, while others may be more comfortable using the phone conference lines. If your software offers users a choice, make sure to test both configurations.

In addition to working out any technical glitches, a practice session will help you determine your pace. Webinars in general run either half-hour or an hour long, depending on the content. Most newcomers to webinars are so worried about filling the time that they may include too much information. Others might have the right amount but will rush the presentation due to nerves. Taking the time to run through the presentation from top to bottom will put you at ease, assuring you have enough time to get your message across and still leave room for questions. For a webinar with around 100 viewers, allow yourself at least 10 minutes for questions. You may want to leave even more time if there is a large audience.

There are several options for how to handle questions. Some webinars will allow users to use their microphone or telephone to ask their questions, while others elect to use a chat feature. In most cases, the chat feature is the best option because you avoid handing over control to a long-winded or very opinionated attendee. You can also skip past questions that you planned to answer later in the presentation. If you can, consider having a coworker monitor the question chat as queries come in to allow you to stay focused on your presentation. That person can also answer the simpler questions or assist with technical concerns. Work out a system to have your coworker interject when questions come in, or ask them all at the end of the presentation. Have your coworker prepare a couple of basic, high-level questions. This will help if there are no questions from the audience and may encourage others to ask questions.

Many webinars take advantage of Twitter's hashtags to encourage real-time feedback through the social network. If you choose this route, it should not be the only option for questions, since not everyone is on Twitter. Have a coworker monitor the search for that keyword, passing along questions to the presenter just as they would any others. Twitter also allows you to continue the conversation after the event ends. Let your users know you will continue to monitor the hashtag to answer any other questions that come up through Twitter. If you get more questions than your time allows, invite attendees to move the conversation online rather than extend the webinar. Be mindful of your attendees' schedules. If they attend a one-hour webinar that ends up lasting 90 minutes, they may be less likely to commit to your next offering.

Getting the most out of your time

The great thing about webinars is that while they only take a finite amount of time to conduct, they can be a marketing asset that brings in leads for months or even years after the event. Most webinar tools allow users to record their sessions, which is another thing to test during your practice time. The recording will capture the same view the live attendees saw, as well as the audio portion. Upload the webinar video to a service like Blip.tv that allows longer presentations, remembering to pick keywords that will attract new users through the site's search tool. Then, embed the video on your blog and promote it just as you did the live webinar. Creating a running list of all your past sessions will eventually lead to a great library of content, especially if you are able to host a session on a schedule, such as monthly or quarterly. This will become a great area to point potential prospects toward for more detail about your products and your company's expertise. You may also elect to upload the slides or other materials to a site like SlideShare, though the viewers will not benefit from your commentary.

Your webinar platform will usually let you know who attended the live session, how long they stayed, if they asked any questions, and in some cases, how attentive they were. It tracks this by monitoring if the user had other windows opened above the webinar viewer. You should use this information to thank your attendees, pointing them to your blog where you plan to archive the session to watch any parts he or she may have missed. In addition to seeing who came, most tools also show you who registered but then did not make the live presentation. Craft a second e-mail for this group, thanking them for registering and pointing them to the same blog post. Make sure you let them know if you are continuing the conversation on Twitter, while also offering to answer any questions they have by e-mail.

KEY TAKEAWAYS

✓	People will listen to an industry expert over a sales person every time, so take steps to increase your personal profile.
✓	Use video to demo products, highlight customer case studies, or as a fun marketing or recruiting tool.
✓	Webinars offer value to your prospects and clients, making users much more likely to attend them than a sales pitch, but avoid the hard sell.
✓	Recording your webinar will give you a resource for years to come.

CHAPTER 10

PR 2.0: Moving Past the Press Release

"Freedom of the press is limited to those who own one."

- A. J. Liebling, contributor to *The New Yorker* magazine

The Internet is responsible for so many changes in the way people do business. Traditional media outlets like newspapers, magazines, television, and radio are no exception. Journalists now have unprecedented access to information that might have taken weeks to sift through on paper. At the same time, they have easy access to hoards of willing sources for their stories. On the flip side, they are also bombarded by e-mails and press releases from marketers and public relations consultants trying to pitch story ideas. Simply writing and distributing a press release is no longer enough to get a story published. Just as the Web has moved to 2.0, so has the media and the public relations industry.

The Paradigm Shift

As recently as 15 years ago, if you had a story to tell, you faxed a press release to an editor or news director at a newspaper or television station. They would look at the merits of the story and trash it or assign it to a reporter to cover. If you had a relationship with a reporter, you could go to them directly to pitch your story. Today's process is completely different, and not just because releases are e-mailed instead of faxed. Reporters have become more accessible. A search online for reporters covering your location or your industry will usually yield sites with lists of names, media outlets, and everything from e-mail addresses to Twitter handles. The result is reporters are overwhelmed with ideas and are forced to delete many without even reviewing them.

At the same time, the process for releasing a pitch on the news wire has become much simpler, with several companies providing the service through a simple Web interface. As a result, the quantity of releases has gone up. Not only that, but the quality of the releases has diminished. Reporters are taught in journalism school to look at what makes a story newsworthy and relevant to their audience. The simple process to distributing releases online has led thousands of companies to push out announcements about everything from a new hire to a new sale — this is hardly newsworthy stuff.

Over this same time, the makeup of the media itself has evolved. Traditional outlets like newspapers that in the past released one edition per day now have reporters posting articles about breaking news as it breaks. Even television stations do not wait for the 6 o'clock news to let their audience know about a story; they use their websites. And do not forget about how the blogosphere has blurred the lines between journalists and the general public. In many cases, getting a blogger — the right blogger — to write about your topic can be just as effective as a newspaper.

Press releases can still drive traffic

It is probably pretty obvious at this point that the traditional press release is not as effective as it once was. There are so many releases to sift through, they are often poorly written or not newsworthy, and thus they are not even making it to the news directors and editors that dictate what gets covered. But that is not to say that press releases have no value. They can be great tools, if not to spark media coverage then to boost your website's search engine rankings and overall traffic.

Remember the search engines' opinions on fresh content. Adding releases to your website, even about things that are not newsworthy enough to make it in the paper or on the news, will have a positive impact the next time your site is indexed. The same rules apply from writing blog posts for search engine optimization: Get your keywords in the title text as well as throughout the release, including text links to other relevant pages on your site. Linking your company's latest news from your site's homepage will help the spiders find them more easily, leading to better rankings for the search terms included on those pages.

Getting your press releases out to other places on the Web can also boost your site's traffic. There are a few free services that will take the work out of distributing your release for you. Rather than submitting your release to all of the search engines, sites like PR Log (**www.prlog.org**) and PressExposure (**www.pressexposure.com**) will get releases out to the major sites like Google News, Yahoo News, and others. Both of those services also allow you to include links within the release for added search engine value, a format known as an **optimized release**.

Some of the wire services mentioned earlier, including PRWeb.com and MarketWire.com, will also send your release out electronically to thousands of media outlets and websites for a price starting at around $200 each. The extra cost includes detailed reporting features not offered with the free tools, though a few online searches can also show you where your release was published. Keep in mind this is still not a very good way to get reporters to pick up your story. What makes these effective is that each article goes out with links embedded back to your site, having a potentially huge impact on your site's inbound links.

Before these releases go out, you are asked to specify what geographic targets you want to focus on, as well as what industries the release is relevant to. Just how many options you can select depends on how much you pay. The releases are then sent to news outlets in the specified locations and to websites covering the industries chosen. Unlike a traditional release, most of these sites do not take the time to evaluate each one. Instead, many will simply import the feed from the distribution company into their website. While it will not be a prominent area of the site — these releases are usually buried on a site — a keyword text link to your company from a major site like MSNBC.com, one of the many sites that carries these releases, still carries plenty of weight.

There are still many sites that will look at the release before blindly listing it on their site, so make sure you take the time to write a good title and summary. Put yourself in your target's shoes by asking yourself if what you have written is newsworthy and relevant to their audience. The wire services keep good statistics on how many people picked up the release, which can help you experiment with different approaches to find the most effective. A sample of the analytics engine for PRWeb can be seen in Figure 65.

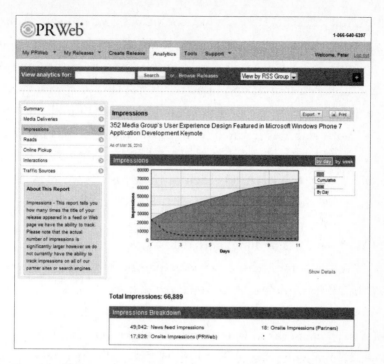

Fig. 65: PRWeb.com's client dashboard breaks down a variety of metrics about a release, including the number of times the title was displayed online.

A HARO Subscription: The Best Free Tool for Marketers Today

Despite all the doom and gloom about how difficult it is to get a reporter's attention, there are still effective and low-cost ways to go about it. They just do not involve press releases. Just as marketers have turned to the Internet to locate publicity opportunities, reporters have started to actively look online for sources. The best and most popular tool available is called Help a Reporter Out™, or **HARO** for short. The free services, started by public relations consultant and author Peter Shankman, makes its money through advertising. It is designed to connect reporters already working on a story with sources who can offer assistance on the given topic.

A very simple concept, HARO gives companies a way to gain immediate media exposure on a daily basis without the costly expense of a public relations retainer. 352 Media Group, for example, went from spending several thousand dollars a month on public relations firms to spending nothing but the time it takes to respond to HARO requests. In under a year, 352 Media Group's staff was featured in blogs and major outlets like *The New York Times, Wall Street Journal, BusinessWeek, Wired, CNNMoney.com*, and more, all directly from HARO. Each of these articles led to phone calls, many from potential clients, though a handful from solicitors.

The HARO service is nothing more than a simple newsletter. Here is how it works: You visit the website (**www.helpareporter.com**) and sign up to receive the notices. You can elect to receive all queries or just those that fall within specific categories. Once registered, you will get three e-mails each business day: one in the morning, one in the afternoon, and the last in the evening. Each e-mail contains a list of requests submitted by members of the media, from bloggers to national television network reporters. They include a summary of the request and, in some cases, the name of the media outlet, but the more prominent outlets tend to keep their names anonymous. Your replies are funneled through the HARO website, so reporters do not have to make their e-mail addresses available to the public. Reporters, usually working on a deadline, will sift through the replies and respond to the ones they would like to interview.

You could also follow @helpareporter on Twitter, as well as become a fan on Facebook. As new requests come in, reporters are asked to include their deadline. If the deadline is within 24 hours, HARO will tweet out the details from that account. Keeping an eye on that account and responding quickly to those requests is a great way to get in front of a reporter desperate for help. They may even remember your helpfulness next time they are working on something related to your business. A reporter is a good friend to have, and one that owes you a favor is even better. Reporters and sources commonly post to the HARO wall on Facebook, linking to stories they wrote or were quoted in, as shown in Figure 66.

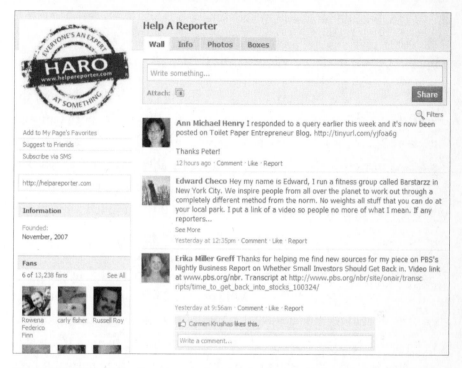

Fig. 66: HARO users are encouraged to share their successes on the company's Facebook page, including links to stories that feature sources from the tool.

Using HARO as a publisher

Submitting a request through the HARO service is not restricted to major media outlets. Posting a request for sources is a great way to beef up a blog post for your company. Take the example of a screen-printing company: Say you are writing a post about the qualities to look for when selecting a screen-printing vendor. Ask for sources who have had problems with your competitors or do-it-yourself alternatives. Also consider using quotes from experts in the industry. The more third-party sources your post includes, the less it will look like a sales pitch. Instead it will look like, and will actually be, a legitimate resource for potential clients. The same can be done when looking for examples to use in a webinar. You may be surprised at how open people are when it comes to free publicity. At the same time, having your blog's name e-mailed out to tens of thousands of registered HARO users could not hurt either.

When to reply

HARO is not a big company, and as a result, not much slips through the cracks. They pride themselves on offering an effective tool to both reporters and sources, and as such, they take abuse seriously. Reporters are encouraged to report off-topic pitches or users taking advantage of the transparency to spam them. Originally, reporters' e-mails were all public. HARO only moved to anonymous e-mail redirects in 2010 to quell attempts by users to copy all the reporter's emails into a database.

What that means for you is only reply when you are confident you are a good fit for the reporter's story. With notifications coming three times a day, often including as many as 50 requests, there is no shortage of opportunity. And there is no reason to take the risk of getting banned from what could be a very valuable resource for your company. There have also been several cases of either reporters or Shankman himself outing abusers via Twitter. When you are a small business looking for good publicity, that is the last thing you need.

Reporters are not looking for press releases, your full biography, or links to marketing materials about your company. They are working on a deadline and need to quickly look at responses to identify a match. This is a good thing for you, since you also want to be very timely in your response, and a more concise reply is quicker to compose. Sticking with the screen printing example, you should watch out for reporter requests specifically about T-shirt printing. However, also keep an eye out for any promotional products, printing technologies, or even general business topics where you can add value to the story. Even if the article is not in a trade publication about screen printing, potential customers may still see it.

When a new query e-mail comes in, scan it right away for opportunities. If you see a match, jump on it quickly. Many reporters will take the first good response they get and ignore the rest, rather than analyzing each e-mail that comes in. So let them know why you are a good fit and briefly give them answers to any questions they asked. In almost every case, the reporter will not use what you write but will contact you for more info. Give them enough to understand that you are a good source for the topic at hand while still providing a thorough response. Given the deadline, you should include as much contact information as you are comfortable with. A reporter will appreciate seeing your mobile number as a sign you are willing to go above and beyond to help.

By staying on top of the e-mails as they come in, you stand a great chance to get some free publicity for your company. HARO users range from individual bloggers up to reporters for the *Wall Street Journal* and ABC's "Good Morning America." They are not just looking to find big executives but instead are often looking for small businesses owners. A connection that would usually cost your company thousands of dollars for a public relations firm's retainer can be free. All you need to do is respond to a couple of e-mails each week.

Other ways to connect with reporters

While HARO is a great way to connect with reporters, it is by no means the only way. In fact, you can use the tools you have already read about, like Twellow or a Facebook search, to find reporters that cover your area or your industry, as well as general assignment reporters from key publications. Not only will you be able to build a relationship by retweeting their posts or commenting on their status, but you will also be notified right away when they write a new article that may interest you. Reporters will often use Twitter to ask for sources when they are on a tight deadline. You may get lucky by following them when they are writing about your industry.

The Role of Blogs in PR 2.0

With some bloggers carrying as much or more weight than traditional media outlets, they should not be overlooked when sending out a release. Without all of the red tape and formality of a newspaper or television station, you may have a better chance connecting with a blog's author. Many make their Twitter and Facebook profiles public, encouraging interaction with readers and sources.

While most people focus on getting a blogger to write about them, there are also opportunities available to write for a blog. Guest posts, which are published stores on blogs from a third-party source, are a common practice. Bloggers may look for guest posts to cover their vacation time or simply to add some variety to the site. When pitching to a blogger, you should consider presenting this option. Look at it from their perspective; they get a new post with fresh content for their site, and they do not have to do any work. In exchange, the blog will usually include a byline with your bio and links to your site. The post itself should not be a sales pitch, but that is not the point. Guest posts are about driving awareness, driving traffic, and improving your status as an industry expert. This is the definition of a win-win situation.

There are a couple of different approaches to take when identifying blogs to pitch. Although their readership may not be as high, you may have more luck going after a smaller blog run by an individual. Chances are they are trying to build their status as well, and therefore they may be interested in the promotion you are willing to offer. In these situations, it is common to offer a guest post opportunity on your company's blog. This way you both leverage each other's networks. You also end up with some fresh, relevant content on your site from a non-competitive source.

Larger blogs, including those with multiple contributors, may be harder to crack. However, the payoff is greater if you do make a deal. Not only would your post get in front or more readers, but you would also benefit more from the links coming from a site with a higher search engine status. These blogs may get several inquiries a day. In fact, many larger blogs may have a section dedicated to guest post submissions. Therefore, it is important to make your pitch stand out. Remember that you are an expert at what you do, so something that you do every day may be interesting to others reading those blogs.

KEY TAKEAWAYS

✓	Do not waste your time spamming news directors and editors with press releases that are not truly newsworthy.
✓	Optimized releases can bring visitors to your site and provide valuable inbound links from sought-after websites.
✓	Register for an account with HARO to find reporters actively looking for experts in your industry.
✓	Do not overlook bloggers, and consider pitching guest posts to blogs that share the same demographics as your company.

WEB 2.0 WORLD

CHAPTER 11

The New Metrics for Measuring Success

"Many of life's failures are people who did not realize how close they were to success when they gave up."

-Thomas A. Edison, American inventor

We have established that Web 2.0 and social media are important, and even if he or she is not sure why or what it is, your boss is likely encouraging you to build the brand online. But after a few months of encouraging you to advantage of all the shiny new features of Web 2.0, he or she will inevitably ask one question: "Is it working?" Your answer may dictate whether you are able to continue these efforts.

Simply saying how many posts you have written, how many times you have tweeted, or even how many fans you have may not be enough. At the end of the day, business owners do not think about how many people saw their product on a store shelf; they do think about how many picked it up. It all boils down to how much revenue was brought in and if that outweighed the cost of time put in to implement these tactics. While retweets, RSS subscribers, and comments are important indicators when evaluating a social media campaign, you need also measure the financial impact to determine the return on investment.

Unless you just stepped in to the marketing role in your company, then you already appreciate the importance of measurement. Everything a marketer does is judged in some way, whether it is clicks, replies, phone calls, or, of course, sales. Direct mail campaigns are assessed on responses, trade shows by leads, and television commercials by brand awareness. What makes Web 2.0 great is that not only should you expect higher return rates, but you can also evaluate them more easily — if you know where to look.

Take a television campaign, for example. You know how many people saw the ad based on the ratings, but even that is not an exact science. It is a figure extrapolated from a small sampling of viewers. And it does not take in to account the viewers' attention. You do not know if they used your commercial's time as a chance to hit the kitchen. And then there are the digital video recorders, letting the audience skip right past your ad. Web-based campaigns, on the other hand, can evaluate all of these things. Not just how many people saw a site or an ad on a site, but how attentive they were, what they did after seeing the ad or social media mention, and if it ultimately brought in a sale. It is just a matter of keeping and evaluating the right metrics.

Metrics Everyone Should Follow

We established in Chapter 3 that the website is the central point that all your online marketing efforts should point to. Therefore, that means it is the biggest thing to evaluate. If your social or other online efforts are working, that will be reflected on the website's traffic statistics. Chapter 4 took a high-level overview of tools like Google Analytics and ClickTracks that take your server logs and put them in a format that is easy to read and analyze. Now it is time to dig deeper and talk about the most important metrics to analyze.

If it is all about the bottom line, then you need to make sure that is measured online. If you manage an e-commerce site where people can make purchases directly, then that is simple. If not, you may still be able to come up with a helpful way to measure the site's effectiveness. Many service companies, for example, are focused around leads. That may mean getting people to pick up the phone or fill out an information request form. In the case of a form, it is just a matter of analyzing the traffic on that page.

Google Analytics lets you set up a special report to track your goals, as shown in Figure 67. There are two main things to look at when evaluating them. The first is the total number of people that visited the goal page, such as your e-commerce checkout page or a request form. The second thing to consider is the relationship of that number to the overall traffic of the site. Determining whether your goal conversion rate is 1 percent or 20 percent will give you a better gauge on where you stand. Take the first few months of your reporting to establish a baseline, and set your targets based on that. As you make changes to your site, monitor the effect they have on these numbers.

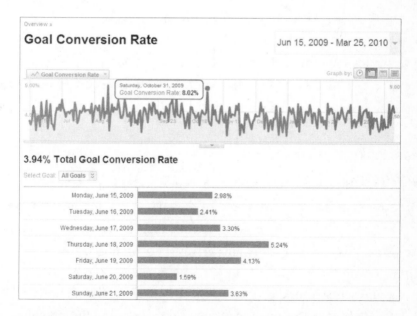

Fig. 67: Your site's goal should be looked at by not only how many users reached it but also the percentage of total visitors that converted, as illustrated on this chart that shows the percentage of 352 Media Group's site visitors who completed a proposal request form.

When you are looking at data related to a request form, you should look at both the traffic for the form page itself, as well the data for the page a user is directed to after completing the form. This often consists of a thank you message, though many sites overlook the importance of this page. Just as e-commerce companies evaluate shopping cart abandonment rates, you should be aware if people are visiting your form but then not filling it out, something you can easily track. Your form should have one Web address while the thank you page, the one a user sees after completing the form, should have a unique address. Comparing the traffic of the two pages will tell you the percentage of people that opt out once they get there. You may find out your form is too long or confusing, resulting in missed opportunities for your company.

Basic social media metrics

While the impact on the bottom line is the most important thing to monitor, it is still good to keep track of the basic social media stats like the number of followers, fans, and connections you have. Watching the correlation between those numbers, the type of content you are providing, and the impact on sales will help you tailor your posts to drive conversions. Here are the numbers to keep track of:

Facebook

- **Fans:** This is the foundation of your Facebook presence. Without fans, your message is not read by anyone, so you monitor this number and ensure it is growing. Remember, however, that attention should be paid to quality fans versus sheer numbers.

- **Comments:** You know your posts are engaging if people are taking the time to comment on them. A comment puts a link to your post on the commenter's wall, so these are a great way to build exposure and, in turn, more fans.

- **Likes:** Think of them as the light version of comments. The result is the same, with your link pushed out to that person's friends.

Twitter

- **Followers:** Just like fans on Facebook, you want to have as many quality followers as possible to give your message the maximum reach.

- **Followers-to-following ratio:** This is an important number that is often overlooked by businesses too focused on building their followers. Many Twitter users look at this ration while deciding whether to follow another user. If you are following far less users than are following you, it is an indication that you are not interested in two-way communication. The opposite ratio says your tweets are not interesting enough to hold on to followers. While the ration does not need to be exactly 1:1, that is a good goal to shoot for. It sends the message that you are interested in what your followers have to say, which is how companies should approach social media.

- **Retweets:** This is equivalent to comments or likes on Facebook and shows that your post is interesting enough to be shared, keeping in mind someone could retweet your post to say they disagree with it. Ask yourself before every tweet whether your post is worth sharing.

- **Mentions:** On Twitter, mentions refer to tweets from other users that mention your username with the @ symbol. This might be someone asking you a question or replying to a question you have posted.

- **Buzz:** Like mentions, buzz refers to any tweets referencing your company or products. Set up searches to keep track of people talking about your company so you can follow them or reply to their questions or concerns.

Blog

- **Views:** In a perfect scenario, your blog exists underneath your main domain name. If this is the case, you can use the same analytics software to keep an eye on your blog's traffic, including the way users enter your main site from your blog. This is especially valuable when judging a blog's worth.

- **Comments:** Comments on your blog do not have the same effect as those on Facebook or Twitter, since they do not inherently mean your post will be seen by that person's network. However, they are still a good sign that your posts and insights are interesting. If nothing else, they serve as new content for your site, which helps keep your site fresh in between new posts.

- **Trackbacks:** While not an exact science by any means, a trackback is an indication that your blog post was mentioned on another blog or website. This is a built-in feature for many popular blogging platforms, while others ask readers to use a specific trackback, or pingback, link when referencing a post. The software does not necessarily catch all references, but looking at the trackbacks from post to post will help you evaluate each post's level of interest.

- **RSS Subscriptions:** Most major blog platforms will let you see a count of people subscribed to the RSS feed from your blog. A subscriber is more than just a casual reader and may be viewing your content in a variety of places from desktop widgets to a content aggregator to a mobile device. Regardless, it is a good metric when evaluating your blog's reach.

Evaluating sentiment

In the case of some of these numbers, more is not necessarily better. Some of the examples in this book have shown how quickly negative comments can spread. That is why it is important to look beyond just the number of posts or tweets about your brand to determine the sentiment behind the post. There are several tools available online at various price points that look for keywords within a post to determine whether it is talking about your company in a positive or negative light.

The simplest tool that looks at emotion is actually part of Twitter's advanced search, online at **http://search.twitter.com/advanced**. It simply looks for tweets with the positive or negative emoticon, :) and :(respectively. You can also search for tweets that include a question mark to find people asking about a particular topic. This is hardly scientific, but other tools take the same premise a little further. Tweetfeel (**www.tweetfeel.com**), for example, provides an even simpler free interface, highlighting words in each tweet as positive or negative. It keeps a running tally of the overall sentiment on the top of the page, as show in Figure 68.

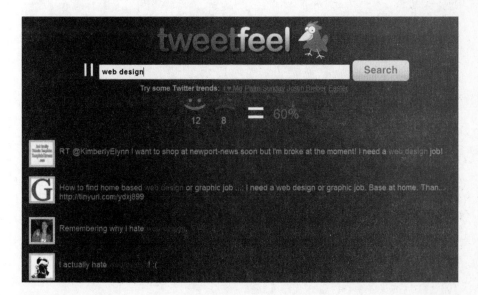

Fig. 68: Tweetfeel.com's interface is simple, yet effective, using happy or sad faces to indicate the mood of each tweet for the term "web design."

Among the more popular tools is Viralheat (**www.viralheat.com**), which includes sentiment analysis in their $29-per-month package. That tool also helps you identify thought leaders within your space to try to engage. Twendz (**www.twendz.com**) offers a free tool that does a basic sentiment analysis. The site allows you to search for a term and see a list of the recent posts as well as a graph showing the percentage of positive, negative, and neutral comments, as show in Figure 69. They also offer a paid service that provides more charting and reporting tools.

Fig. 69: The left side of Twendz shows other topics related to your search while the graph on the bottom illustrates how sentiment changes over time, in this case over the previous four-hour period.

Metrics to Follow to Get Promoted

Looking at the basic numbers will give you a good overview of the effectiveness of your social media and other Web 2.0 efforts. Tying those numbers to an impact on sales, however, is where you can really see the power of online marketing. Many tactics for tracking an offline campaign's return on investment simply look at the correlation of advertising to sales over a campaign's life cycle, ignoring other influencers like the economy or the actions of your competition — these can have a significant impact on those numbers. Campaigns do not exist in a vacuum, void of other influencers. On the other hand, Web tools can help you actually prove causation between advertising and sales.

Olivier Blanchard, author and blogger at **www.thebrandbuilder.wordpress.com**, is an outspoken believer in the ability to track social media's effectiveness for marketing. Blanchard advocates the F.R.Y. (frequency, reach, yield) method as a great way to evaluate social media return on investment. You should be able to get the buy-in you need in order to continue your efforts by proving the impact of your campaign in these key areas.

Frequency deals with shortening the time between purchases. The argument is that by staying on your customer's radar through various social media channels, they may be more likely to buy more often. This is a very easy number to pull if your company deals with repeat business in a way that is attributed directly to the individual, like an e-commerce website. For example, a site can track the amount of time between when a customer makes a purchase. A coffee shop, on the other hand, would need to implement a loyalty program in order to tie a particular purchase to a specific customer.

In this method, reach has two meanings. The first is the obvious goal of most advertising campaigns to reach more prospects. Sticking with the example of an e-commerce website, this can be measured by looking at the change in the number of different customers who made purchases compared to the same time period before the social campaign got underway. The second way to look at reach is in relation to your other products. Social media, in addition to bringing in more customers, can also help existing ones reach further into your product line. Say you have a Facebook page dedicated to fans of a particular product. Now you can suggest complimentary products like accessories or service contracts to those users, leveraging your existing client base to expand your reach.

The final measure is yield. This looks at the average dollar amount per sale. What you are really looking at here is the brand loyalty over the life of your relationship with a client. This extends beyond simply shortening the sales cycle, looking more at the value of each transaction. Getting someone who normally buys one product per transaction to buy two or three will have a big impact on the bottom line. This may include encouraging users of a basic product to upgrade to a more advanced pro version.

Determining what constitutes a financial impact

All of the social media metrics covered earlier in the chapter are important, but none of them are tied directly to your company's financials. They are stepping stones that will eventually lead to your campaign's success or failure. However, walking into the boss's office with a chart showing your rise in followers likely will not get the reaction you would hope for. Instead, you will be asked the simple question: "But how did that affect sales?" The first thing to do is understand what your hard costs are.

It is easy to look at social media as a free marketing tool. Unlike a billboard or hiring a skywriter, a Facebook page costs you nothing out of pocket. It is a common mistake to overlook the impact these campaigns have on your time. Unlike a direct mail piece, where the drag on your time ends after the mail goes out, social media marketing requires constant attention. You cannot simply create a page and then hand control over to the sales team to work the leads. A blog without new content is a waste of resources, while an outdated fan page on Facebook will reflect poorly on your brand.

Now that you have identified your hard costs, it is time to determine your financial goals. Every marketing campaign, online or otherwise, needs to do one of two things: reduce costs or increase revenue. While there is an increase on your time to implement social media marketing efforts, there may also be a reduction of other hard costs that come with it. You may be able to replace that billboard that costs you $5,000 a month with a Twitter account that reaches as many people. While so many marketers are focused on the sales impact of their work, it is easy to overlook the cost savings afforded by social media. In order to be able to justify your work, you need to keep a tally of your fixed marketing expenses, looking at the value of your time as well as the cost to your vendors.

The vast majority of marketing is focused on driving higher revenue. Looking back at the F.R.Y. method, that may include increasing the value or regularity of sales per customer, introducing new products to existing clients, or reaching out to new clients altogether. Social media and Web 2.0 can also have a significant impact on these goals, by being both less expensive than comparable traditional marketing and easier to monitor. However in order to judge the effectiveness, you need to have all of the relevant data.

Establishing a starting point

You cannot know where you are headed without a clear understanding of where you have been. This means understanding your baselines for website traffic, social media buzz, and your number of followers and fans. It also means tracking your overall sales, sales by customer or by segment, and the average value of each sale. Try to gather as much of this historical data as you can before starting your campaign. The more data, the better, because you can see the overall trends rather than just the ebb and flow of sales that may happen from day to day.

Now that you have your baseline, and hopefully several prior months of data, it is time to start the campaign. The easiest thing to do would be to come back once the marketing campaign is over and compare the numbers over the previous period. That is a typical approach with offline marketing, but remember that there is so much more data to look at when it comes to Web 2.0. For starters, keep a running timeline of important milestones that take place during the campaign. This is where the basic social media metrics come in to play. For example, mark down on the timeline what day you wrote a new blog post. Also record things like retweets or Facebook comments from industry influencers. Keep a running list in a document or spreadsheet that you keep on your desktop for easy access.

Here is where the work finally starts to pay off. Take the timeline and overlay it with all your other information. Your chart may look something like the example in Figure 70, which shows the relationships between the changes in the various financial and social metrics. The vertical line is the marker for when the social media campaign started, which explains the jump in followers, fans, and website traffic in the second half of the year. Rather than simply showing a sales increase or an uptick in social media metrics, you should show how one impacts the other.

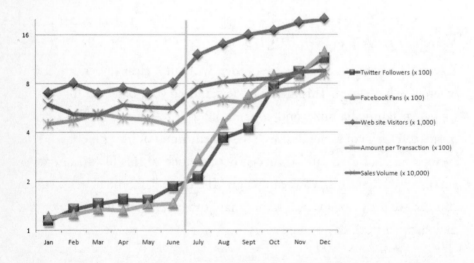

Fig. 70: Placing your sales numbers on top of your social metrics gives a better indication of the relationship between the two numbers.

Figure 70, while impressive, still does not prove the social media marketing was the reason for the sales and per transaction boosts. This is nearly impossible without polling your customers, which may not be feasible in every case. This is where the social media timeline is important. Take a look at the chart in Figure 71, which shows just the data gathered after the campaign started. Key points from the timeline are included, allowing you to see the impact, if any, of each blog post, each tweet, and each influencer's retweet. Make sure to include the negative as well. This data is what you will use to make your next campaign better, so you need to understand the impact of what went right as well as what went wrong.

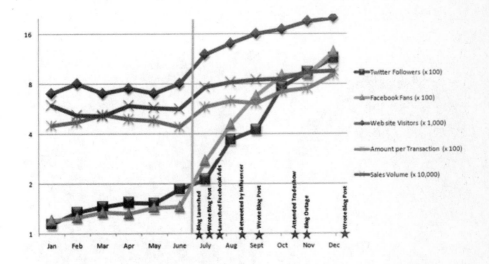

Fig. 71: Look at your milestones alongside your numbers to get an idea for how each this affected your return on investment after your campaign started, the point representing by the vertical line.

Some businesses sell products both online and in retail stores or through wholesale channels. Therefore, it is important to measure the impact of your social media marketing campaign across all aspects of your company. Someone may have seen your special on Facebook but took advantage of it in your store. This is why exclusive campaigns for different mediums can be so helpful to tracking. If you only posted that promotion on Facebook, then you are able to track its success regardless of how the customer made the purchase. The last thing you need is someone else taking credit for your work.

KEY TAKEAWAYS

✓	Mood matters. A tweet about your company is not always a good thing, so keep track of the sentiment online.
✓	Focus on the financials, but do not ignore the other indicators. They are important steps that get you to your monetary goals.
✓	Do not wait until your campaign starts to start measuring. You need data to compare to.
✓	Look at everything in context. Look at how each number affects the next.

CONCLUSION

In the time it took you to read this book, whether it was a couple of weeks or a couple of hours, things have already changed. Your company or industry may have been mentioned on Twitter. A competitor may have joined Facebook. An entirely new social network, maybe even the next big phenomenon, may have popped up online. Trying to keep up with everything is impossible. Instead, identify the areas where you can have the most impact and get the biggest return for your efforts. At the same time, be careful not to dismiss any new trends. More than a few businesses scoffed at Twitter when it first came on the scene. A myopic view can be a big disadvantage when it comes to marketing your company online.

And finally, be yourself. I have harped on this point time and time again, not only because it is important, but also because of how many businesses have fallen short in this area. People go online to connect with other people. Even in a B2B environment, users expect a personality from others on Twitter and Facebook. There is a reason they are called social networks. Have fun, be social, and get the word out. When done the right way, something that you now know how to do, Web 2.0 can boost your brand to become a recognized leader among your audience; that, of course, means a boost on the bottom line. And is that not the point?

APPENDIX

Resources

Content Management Systems			
Service	**Website**	**Description**	**Cost**
Movable Type	**www.movable-type.org**	A community effort, led by Six Apart, devoted to building and maintaining the open source version of Movable Type.	Free
Drupal	**www.drupal.org**	Allows an individual or a community of users to publish, manage, and organize a variety of website content.	Free
OpenCMS	**www.opencms.org**	Based on Java and XML technology; can be used in an open-source environment (Linux, Apache, Tomcat, MySQL),as well as on commercial components (Windows NT, IIS, BEA Weblogic, Oracle).	Free

Ektron	www.ektron.com	Provides a complete platform with all of the functionality necessary to create, deploy, and manage website content.	$7,200 per license
Microsoft SharePoint	http://sharepoint2007.microsoft.com	Provides comprehensive content management and enterprise search, accelerating shared business processes, and facilitating information sharing across boundaries.	Express: Free Office SharePoint Server 2007 for Internet Sites: $41,134
352 Media Group's CMS	www.352media.com/Content-Management.aspx	Can edit and create text, add hyperlinks, add pictures, insert tables, create anchor tags, and so much more; can even add new Web pages and update menu bars.	License: Free Installation & customization: from $1,600

Forums			
Service	**Website**	**Description**	**Cost**
MyBB	www.mybbboard.net	A professional and efficient discussion board developed by an active team of developers.	Free
Telligent Community	www.telligent.com	Enables you to listen to, learn from, and improve conversations with customers, partners, and prospects.	From $6,000

Newsletters and E-mail Promotions			
Service	**Website**	**Description**	**Cost**
MailChimp	**www. mailchimp.com**	Can send e-mail news-letters to customers, manage subscriber lists, and track campaign performance.	Up to 500 sub-scribers/3,000 e-mails per month: Free Up to 2,500 subscribers/ unlimited e-mails: $30/ month
Constant Contact	**www.constant-contact.com**	Offers e-mail market-ing, online survey, and event marketing tools.	Up to 500 subscribers/ unlimited e-mails: $15/ month Up to 25,000 subscribers/ unlimited e-mails: $150/ month
352 Media Group's HTML News-letter and E-mail Blaster	**www. 352media. com/HTML-Newsletter-EmailBlaster. aspx**	Can develop HTML e-mail newsletter templates that keep in line with the theme and brand of your website; will monitor the suc-cess of each campaign to see bounce-backs or unsubscribes, as well as how many people opened your e-mails and what links they clicked.	License: $2,495 plus hosting

Polls/surveys			
Service	**Website**	**Description**	**Cost**
Survey Monkey	**www.survey-monkey.com**	Founded in 1999, SurveyMonkey is the world's leading provider of web-based survey solutions. Powerful, yet easy-to-use, Survey-Monkey helps millions of people gain the insights they need to make more informed decisions.	Free to $19.95/month
Constant Contact	**www.constant-contact.com**	Offers insightful online surveys and begin a dialogue with their customers.	Up to 5,000 survey responses: $15/month 5,000 or more responses: $0.05 per response
352 Media Group's Polls and Surveys	**www. 352media. com/PollsSur-veys.aspx**	We understand the importance of knowing your customer and the best way to do that is to ask. Surveys can be grouped together for clients hoping to offer advice or help. Results are logged and can be retrieved at any point.	License: $1,495 plus hosting

Blog Platforms			
Service	**Website**	**Description**	**Cost**
Blogger	**www.blogger. com**	Now owned by Google; focuses on helping people have their own voice to organize the world's information.	Free
WordPress. com	**www.word- press.com**	A hosted version of the open-source pack- age where you can start a blog in seconds without any technical knowledge.	Free
WordPress. org	**www.word- press.org**	Publishing platform with a focus on aes- thetics, Web stan- dards, and usability.	Free license, plus hosting
TypePad	**www.typepad. com**	Allows you to add con- tent, pictures, and links quickly	$8.95/month to $89.95/month
352 Media Group's Blog Platform	**http:// new.352media. com/Blog-wm. aspx**	Joined with BlogEn- gine.net to offer a platform to interact and communicate with the world.	License and set up: $1,995, plus hosting

Analytics			
Service	**Website**	**Description**	**Cost**
Google Analytics	**www.google. com/analytics**	Gives you insights into your website traffic and marketing effectiveness; lets you see and analyze your traffic data in an entirely new way.	Free
Clicktale	**www.clicktale. com**	See where your visitors are coming from and watch what they are doing in real time.	$99/month to $790/month
Webtrends	**www.webt-rends.com**	Helps turn your data into understanding of your customers and business opportunity.	$1,556 per 1 million annual page views

Surveillance Tools			
Service	**Website**	**Description**	**Cost**
Google Alerts	**www.google. com/alerts**	E-mail updates of the latest relevant Google results based on your topic choice.	Free
Google Reader	**www.google. com/reader**	Keeps track of all the sites you visit in one, manageable page.	Free
Boardreader	**www.boar-dreader.com**	Connects communities through searches.	Free
Social Mention	**www.social-mention.com**	Receive daily e-mail alerts of your brand, company, CEO, marketing campaign, developing news story, or a competitor.	Free

Twitter Clients			
Service	**Website**	**Description**	**Cost**
Ping.fm	**www.ping.fm**	Allows you to update all of your social networks at once.	Free
TweetDeck	**www.tweetdeck. com**	Helps organize your contacts across Twitter, Facebook, MySpace, LinkedIn, and more.	Free
Hootsuite	**Hootsuite www.hootsuite. com**	Manages multiple users over various social network accounts.	Free

Video Platforms			
Service	**Website**	**Description**	**Cost**
YouTube	**www.youtube. com**	Allows people to discover, watch, and share originally-created videos; acts as a distribution platform for original content creators and advertisers large and small.	Free
Blip.tv	**www.blip.tv**	Independent show creators are great at making content. They are great at technology, business development, distribution, and advertising sales.	Free
DailyMotion	**www.dailymotion.com**	Allows you to find or upload videos on any topic.	Free
Metacafe	**www.metacafe. com**	Makes it easy to find videos from your favorite content creators.	Free

Screen Recorders

Service	Website	Description	Cost
AutoScreen-Recorder	www.wisdom-soft.com	Allows you to record video file or Flash movie.	Free to $49.95
Camtasia	www.techsmith.com	Allows you to create videos that train, teach, sell, and more.	$299

Webinar Platforms

Service	Website	Description	Cost
GoToWebinar	www.gotowebi-nar.com	Can conduct do-it-yourself webinars with up to 1,000 people.	$99/month to $499/month
ReadyTalk	www.readytalk.com	Offers Web and audio conferencing.	$0.20 per user per minute
Webex	www.webex.com	Allows you to deliver engaging multimedia events to multiple computer screens.	$0.33 per user per minute
Adobe Connect	www.adobe.com/products/acrobatconnectpro	Allows you to share presentations and multimedia right from your desktop and get feedback from hundreds of participants; already installed on more than 98 percent of Internet-connected personal computers.	$0.32 per user per minute to $55/month

Press Release Distribution			
Service	**Website**	**Description**	**Cost**
PRWeb	www.prweb.com	Distributes news and press releases to raise your online visibility.	From $80 per release
Marketwire	www.marketwire.com	Offers press release distribution, media contact management, multimedia, media monitoring services, and other workflow solutions.	From $140 per release
PR Log	www.prlog.com	An online press release distribution and submission service.	Free
Press Exposure	www.pressexposure.com	Allows companies, organizations, and individuals to submit press releases.	Free
PRBuzz	www.prbuzz.com	Offers unlimited distribution.	$299/year for unlimited releases

GLOSSARY

Application-programming interface (API): A tool that allows developers to build on top of a platform by accessing certain content.

Blog roll: A list of other blogs that complement your own and are linked from your blog.

Blog: Originally short for Weblog; a site that is essentially an online journal.

Body text: The main content areas of your website that are not titles or links.

Bounce rate: The percentage of visitors who left your site after visiting only one page.

Cascading style sheets (CSS): Classes within a site's code that ensure the design elements of the site are maintained; they control font styles, text sizes, colors, and other parameters for different categories of content.

Comment spam: Blog comments that are not submitted as a legitimate response to the post, but rather to promote another link.

Completely Automated Public Turing test to tell Computers and Humans Apart (CAPTCHA): Usually consists of an additional field on a form where the user is asked to respond to a challenge question to confirm he or she is human.

Contact forms: A series of questions used to gather feedback or contact information from a website's user.

Content management systems (CMS): Web-based software that lets you add, edit, or delete content in select areas of any page on the website with no knowledge of HTML or other coding languages.

Crawl cycle: The time between each visit from a spider.

Deep crawl: An exhaustive indexing of every page a spider can find on a site.

Direct message (DM): A tweet that is only visible to the intended recipient, which, depending on the recipient's settings, may be sent to his or her e-mail account.

E-mail newsletters: An electronic version of a printed newsletter that is sent to a subscriber's inbox.

Embed code: HTML code provided by a website that lets a user embed content like video or audio within another site.

Emoticons: Textual representations of facial expressions.

Forums: Tools that let visitors post questions or comments that can be commented on by other users, including your company's employees.

Fresh crawl: A more frequent crawl focused on those pages the search engines identify as being updated more often.

Hashtags: # + keyword; Often used by tweeters to indicate that their post is about a particular topic.

Help a Reporter Out (HARO): A free service designed to connect reporters already working on a story with sources who can offer assistance on the given topic.

Inbound links: Links from third-party sites that link to your website.

Keyword density: The amount of times a keyword is used on a particular Web page or site.

Keywords: The terms used by someone searching for a website.

Landing pages: Not always the homepage; the page through which a user enters your site.

Link text: Any plain text on your site that links to another page, either on your site or externally.

Marketing mix: The main factors of marketing; comprised of product, price, placement, promotion, and people.

Marketing myopia: The lack of foresight businesses often suffer from when looking at their own products of services.

Metadata: The specific code a website developer uses to describe the site in its HTML.

Optimized release: A press release designed for Web distribution that includes text links to your site.

Organic ranking: Determined by each search engine; the order of the most relevant content for a particular search query.

Pay per click: An auction-style system for placement on the search engines under certain keywords where the company is only charged if its link is clicked.

Polls: Any one-answer question posed by a website to its users; multiple-questions constitute a survey.

Pull/inbound marketing: A customer-driven, passive approach to marketing based on building awareness.

Push/outbound marketing: Often called direct or interruption marketing; includes promotions like television commercials and magazine advertisements.

Really simple syndication (RSS): An industry-standard platform used to publish content that is constantly being updated, such as blogs, news headlines, and even audio and video.

Relationship marketing: Marketing that relies on direct interaction with customers.

Retweet: A tweet that is a rehash of another user's post, often with comments added.

Sandbox: The holding area where new sites go before they make it in to the search results.

Social media: A broad term that describes websites or tools made up of primarily user-generated content that foster interaction between users.

Social networks: Any website that connects users and allows them to share information directly.

Spidering (crawling): The process used by search engines to scan the Web and create a record of what they have discovered.

Sponsored conversations: Refers to paid blog posts masquerading as editorial content.

Title text: A section header within the site's content area or the overall page title that displays in the Web browser's header.

Tweet: A post on Twitter, a micro-blogging service.

Web 2.0: A term used to describe interactive websites and tools that promote two-way conversations.

Webinars: Web-based seminars or tutorials.

BIBLIOGRAPHY

Brogan, Chris and Julien Smith. *Trust Agents: Using the Web to Build Influence, Improve Reputation, and Earn Trust.* John Wiley and Sons, Inc. 2009.

Buchanan, R. and Gilles, C. "Value managed relationship: The key to customer retention and profitability." European Management Journal, Vol. 8(4) . 1990.

Godin, Seth. Meatball Sundae: *Is Your Marketing Out of Sync?* Piatkus Books. 2008.

Halligan, Brian and Shah Dharmesh. *Inbound Marketing: Get Found Using Google, Social Media, and Blogs.* John Wiley and Sons, Inc. 2009.

Olivier Blanchard Basics Of Social Media ROI, **www.slideshare.net/the-brandbuilder/olivier-blanchard-basics-of-social-media-roi**. Accessed April 2010.

Reichheld, F. and Sasser, W. (1990) "Zero defects: quality comes to services." Harvard Business Review, Sept–Oct. 1990.

Scott, David Meerman. *The New Rules of Marketing and PR: How to Use Social Media, Blogs, News Releases, Online Video, and Viral Marketing to Reach Buyers Directly.* John Wiley and Sons, Inc. 2010.

Scott, David Meerman. *World Wide Rave: Creating Triggers that Get Millions of People to Spread Your Ideas and Share Your Stories.* John Wiley and Sons, Inc. 2009.

BIOGRAPHY

Peter VanRysdam was a telecommunications major at the University of Florida where he met his business partner, Geoff Wilson, in 1996. While still a student, VanRysdam was asked to join the 352 Media Group team while it was still in its infancy. As head of the sales department, he helped the company quickly grow into a significant player in the Web design and development market by landing several of the company's larger accounts, including Knight Ridder (now The McClatchy Company), Monterey Boats, and Microsoft.

VanRysdam has worn many hats in his tenure with the company and has now focused on his passion as the chief marketing officer. In this role, he sets the direction for and manages the implementation of all aspects of the company's marketing efforts, including everything from search engine marketing to viral campaigns to 352's own website. In addition, he still works directly with a handful of 352 Media Group's most significant client relationships, including Microsoft in Seattle, Washington. VanRysdam has spoken at several industry events, including social media summits for the

American Marketing Association. He also conducts frequent webinars on topics ranging from website usability to blogging best practices.

When he is not at 352 Media Group, VanRysdam sits on the board of HOPE, an equine-assisted therapy nonprofit in north Florida. In his spare time, he enjoys playing softball, playing music, and spending time with his wife, Megan, his daughter, Abigail, and their two Jack Russell terriers. The family often has a full house, as they are active participants in the Alachua County Humane Society's foster program, as well as several other local pet rescues.

INDEX

WEB 2.0 WORLD

S

T

U

V

W

Y